Martha Stewart's
NEWLYWED KITCHEN

Martha Stewart's
NEWLYWED KITCHEN

Recipes for Weeknight Dinners & Easy, Casual Gatherings

**From the Editors of
Martha Stewart Living
Photographs by Stephen Kent Johnson**

Clarkson Potter/Publishers
New York

Published in the United States by Clarkson Potter/Publishers,
an imprint of the Crown Publishing Group, a division of Penguin
Random House LLC, New York.
crownpublishing.com
clarksonpotter.com
marthastewart.com

CLARKSON POTTER is a trademark and POTTER with colophon is
a registered trademark of Penguin Random House LLC.

Library of Congress Cataloging-in-Publication Data
Names: Stewart, Martha. | Martha Stewart Living Omnimedia.
Title: Martha Stewart's newlywed kitchen: recipes for weeknight
dinners & easy, casual gatherings / editors of Martha Stewart
Living.
Other titles: Newlywed kitchen | Martha Stewart living.
Description: New York : Clarkson Potter, [2016] | Includes index.
Identifiers: LCCN 2016034449| ISBN 9780307954381
(hardcover : alk. paper) | ISBN 9780307954398 (ebook)
Subjects: LCSH: Dinners and dining. | Entertaining. |
LCGFT: Cookbooks.
Classification: LCC TX737 .M3795 2016 | DDC 641.5/4—dc23
LC record available at https://lccn.loc.gov/2016034449

ISBN 978-0-307-95438-1
Ebook ISBN 978-0-307-95439-8

Printed in China

Book and cover design by Michael McCormick
Photographs by Stephen Kent Johnson

10 9 8 7 6 5 4 3 2 1

First Edition

TO COUPLES EVERYWHERE: RECIPES FOR A
GOOD LIFE TOGETHER, FOREVER

CONTENTS

FOREWORD

Getting married is exciting. Getting married is exhilarating. Yet getting married presents every couple with challenges both large and small, and it is generally agreed that every couple can use all the support and reinforcement that the rest of us can offer. Our newest cookbook is designed with the recently married in mind. It provides delightful and delicious solutions for one of a couple's most frequently discussed topics: what to have for dinner.

Prior to the wedding day, everything may seem so much simpler: Dinner can be on the run; it can be at a favorite hangout, a new restaurant, out with friends. After marriage, however, a new reality sets in: Dinner for two becomes the accepted—and expected—norm, and inviting others to your dinner table occurs more frequently. How to please, what to serve, how to entertain, who to invite, what to make for dessert—these thoughts and questions abound. After a few decades of creating thousands of recipes for home cooks at every level, we, the food editors of Martha Stewart Living, know what works and what doesn't work. We understand the way people like to cook and to eat on ordinary weeknights, weekends, holidays, and special occasions. We know the recipes that appeal, the preparations that please, and we have compiled in this beautifully photographed book more than one hundred recipes that will get you through any meal, confidently, with ease and aplomb.

And lest you think that this book is meant to be consulted and relied upon only in the first few years of marriage, rest assured, it is not. In the course of compiling, testing, tasting, and photographing the many wonderful dishes within, we found it to be a book for all of us, regardless of stage of life or marital status. We rediscovered a few old favorites, fell hard for some new ones, and grew excited at the many possibilities for memorable breakfasts, brunches, lunches, dinners, and desserts. Like any good marriage, this collection is built to last.

Martha Stewart

PART ONE

STOCK UP

———

11
NEWLYWED
KITCHEN

You and your partner may have different cooking styles, different skill sets, different ideas about what dinner means ("what—no meat?"), and even different approaches to entertaining. And depending on the size of your kitchen, it can be challenging to work side by side, especially at the end of a long day. But your kitchen is likely to become the heart of your home— the source of many delicious victories as well as a few epic fails (otherwise known as teachable moments).

Whether the two of you are novices or longtime cooks, you may be merging two kitchens into one and are likely adding wedding gifts to the mix. Now is an excellent time to assess the contents of your collective kitchen and decide how you want to outfit it. And even if you've been cooking together for years, it pays to adopt a new game plan. After all, cooking as a couple— or alone for that matter—is almost always better in a well-stocked kitchen. That doesn't mean you need a giant space filled with top-of-the-line equipment and the latest gadgets. It just means that before you get started, you should take stock. And then stock up—or pare down, as the case may be.

What's the best way to build a collection of kitchenware? Most chefs suggest accumulating things slowly, rather than all at once. Consider how you like to cook and how much storage you have before you invest in whole sets. A great place to start is with an ovenproof, straight-sided, 10- or 12-inch skillet; you can sear, pan-fry, or braise small cuts of meat, roast a chicken, sauté vegetables, or make a frittata in it.

Storage space is important, too, when deciding whether or not to add small appliances—say, a blender, juicer, food processor, or espresso machine—to your kitchen. Choose those that will fit your current needs (the two of you, primarily) and your cabinets. Start with just the basics, and add more only if the need arises. If you're not a big baker, for example, you probably don't need a stand mixer living on the counter.

Invest in the best-quality knives, pots, and pans you can afford. Using a thin-bottomed pot for cooking rice may cause you to scorch it, and a dull knife is guaranteed to make chopping a chore (and more hazardous, too). That said, becoming a better, more versatile cook doesn't have to involve great expense. An offset spatula, box grater, and sturdy peeler all cost next to nothing, and they handle multiple kitchen tasks.

Opt for tools that can do double duty as much as possible, instead of buying specialty ones. A sieve, for example, can stand in for a flour sifter, and a rimmed baking sheet turned upside down works as an improvised pizza peel. You don't need a garlic peeler when you can use the flat side of a chef's knife to split the skins. Before you know it, the two of you will have everything you need at hand to make cooking together easier— and more fun.

KITCHEN TEAMWORK

A home-cooked meal is an enduring symbol of comfort—for good reason. Not only does it nourish you, but it can also nourish any relationship. Getting dinner on the table may feel challenging, especially when you're both on the go from sun up to sun down. The solution: teamwork. Cook together and you'll soon be enjoying a streamlined, efficient process for those delicious weeknight meals.

Being able to navigate the kitchen as a team is an invaluable skill to share. When you're apart during the day, joining forces to cook dinner is a good opportunity to reconnect and share stories. As a bonus, choosing recipes, negotiating who does what, troubleshooting when things go awry, and, ultimately, enjoying the fruits of your collective labor will boost your communication skills and improve your power as a pair.

There's another compelling reason to cook in tandem: Research has shown that happy couples regularly experience new things together (e.g., taking a painting class, discovering a new neighborhood). Learning to cook—with the wide variety of techniques, infinite recipes, and limitless flavor profiles— basically guarantees a lifetime of new experiences. Add to that the fact that home-cooked meals are generally healthier and less expensive, and you have every reason to commit to cooking together.

And don't worry if it's not all smooth sailing. When you and your partner merge your kitchens and start preparing meals side by side, there are bound to be moments when you step on each other's toes (sometimes quite literally) and unknowingly break each other's rules. The good news is those moments are usually avoidable. Here are some tips for dividing and conquering.

Follow the leader.
Do what restaurants do and institute a hierarchy in the kitchen: Assign a chef and a sous chef. A sous chef follows the chef's directions and assists with whatever needs to be done, whether it's chopping onions or stirring the soup. If you naturally prefer to call the shots or are the more experienced cook, you may want to take the lead.

Take turns.
Here's the thing: Who wears which hat can change, depending on your moods, energy levels, or who chose the meal, and that's a good thing. You should swap roles as often as you like.

Sort by strengths.
Are you the one with the knife skills? Does your partner love making salads? Play to your proficiencies. Leave the rice to the risotto whisperer and assign the lasagna to whoever is better at layering. The point is, sometimes everyone's happier (and meals turn out tastier) when you're each in your own comfort zone.

Consider who cleans.
If you're an adamant non-cook and can't be persuaded to pick up a knife, you can still be involved in kitchen activities. Wash dirty pots, wipe counters, and prep dishes as your partner does the cooking. Some people prefer to clean up all at once, after the meal, but no one is going to complain if some of the dishwashing gets done before you eat. (And, yes, it's also your responsibility to set the table and clean the dishes post-meal.)

Create a playbook before hosting.
Having people over for dinner? The division of labor just got a little more complicated. In addition to figuring out who handles what in the kitchen (and when), you'll also need to add a few tasks to the to-do list: choosing music, greeting guests, taking coats, pouring drinks, replenishing food, and clearing plates. The key is to communicate clearly, assign tasks beforehand, and have fun.

PREP TOOLS

Almost every recipe begins with prepping ingredients. Stock up on these basic tools, which perform a host of small but important jobs, and your cooking prep should be a breeze.

1. Ice cream scoop
Think beyond ice cream. Use this to measure out cookie dough, cupcake or muffin batter, or meatball mix. Look for a weighted, easy-to-grip handle; some models have defrosting liquid sealed inside, which is activated by the warmth of your hand, but a quick run under warm water does the trick, too.

2. Mixing bowls
When stainless-steel mixing bowls—standard issue in restaurant kitchens—became readily available to every home cook, life got a lot easier. They're nonreactive to acidic ingredients, non-breakable, and inexpensive. An easy-pour spout for liquids is a user-friendly tweak.

3. Nesting bowls
You can never have too many multipurpose (and heatproof!) bowls. They come in a range of just-right sizes, so you're never at a loss, whether you need to assemble ingredients for smoothies, improvise a double-boiler, or whisk dry ingredients for baking projects. A set that nests neatly offers efficient storage.

4. Measuring spoons
Genius lies in the details: An inexpensive set of measuring spoons can take the guesswork out of eyeballing a teaspoon of this and a tablespoon of that. Look for those made from stainless steel, which won't bend, snap, or warp.

5. Dry-measuring cups
Measuring accurately—the unsung building block to success in the kitchen—isn't hard when you know how. Spoon dry ingredients (flour and sugar) as well as semisolid ones (peanut butter) into nesting cups (typically made of metal or plastic) that can be leveled off with a straight edge.

6. Box grater
An all-purpose, four-sided box grater is definitely worth having: Freshly grated cheese elevates almost any pasta dish, pizza, or green salad. Look for a box grater that's stable and comfortable to use; non-slip rubber around the bottom helps you make quick work of grating cabbage for slaw, as well as carrots and other root vegetables. If storage is at a premium, look for a single-sided or collapsible variety.

7. Plastic cutting boards
Among the essential tools for slicing, dicing, and chopping are cutting boards. Those made of a nonporous plastic are solid and durable yet relatively soft, so they won't dull your knife. Stock a few in various sizes and designate them accordingly, to keep ingredients such as raw poultry and vegetables separate.

8. Mandoline
An adjustable-blade slicer is another tool that has made the jump from professional kitchens to the home front, and it's easy to understand why: It makes even, thin slices and ribbons of hard vegetables and fruits, for things like scalloped potatoes or baked vegetable chips. A solid, stable, plastic version is less intimidating, less expensive, and takes up less room than a larger, heavier stainless-steel one.

9. Mortar and pestle
This ancient kitchen tool is just as satisfying to use as it was thousands of years ago. Try pounding spices and garlic for pastes and rubs in a small ceramic or marble one; you can also grind whole peppercorns or other spices in lieu of a pepper mill or electric grinder. (And do get in the habit of grinding your own spices; they taste so much fresher.) Larger sizes are more practical for pesto (its name comes from this tool) and guacamole.

10. Wooden cutting board
Resilient and shock absorbent, wood is an all-time great cutting surface, and its warmth and beauty add charm to any kitchen. Use it for prepping or as a serving piece for cheeses or charcuterie.

11. Liquid-measuring cup
This lets you check the level of a liquid at eye level. The heat-proof glass is hard to break and easy to clean. (We can't say this enough, however: Use it *only* for liquid ingredients.)

12. Rasp
Using a super-sharp rasp to grate cheese, citrus zest, chocolate, or whole nutmeg makes these kitchen chores much more efficient and fast. Cleanup is a cinch, too. Fun fact: This tool was originally designed for woodworking.

13. Peeler
In your kitchen arsenal of sharp tools, nothing works harder than the humble peeler. The wider blade of a Y-shaped peeler works especially well on winter squash and other thicker-skinned vegetables. You can also use it to cut zucchini, cucumbers, or carrots into ribbons.

14. Lemon/lime press
This Mexican-style press works by turning a lemon or lime half inside out and pressing out juice and essential oils. It's the easiest, most efficient tool for the job.

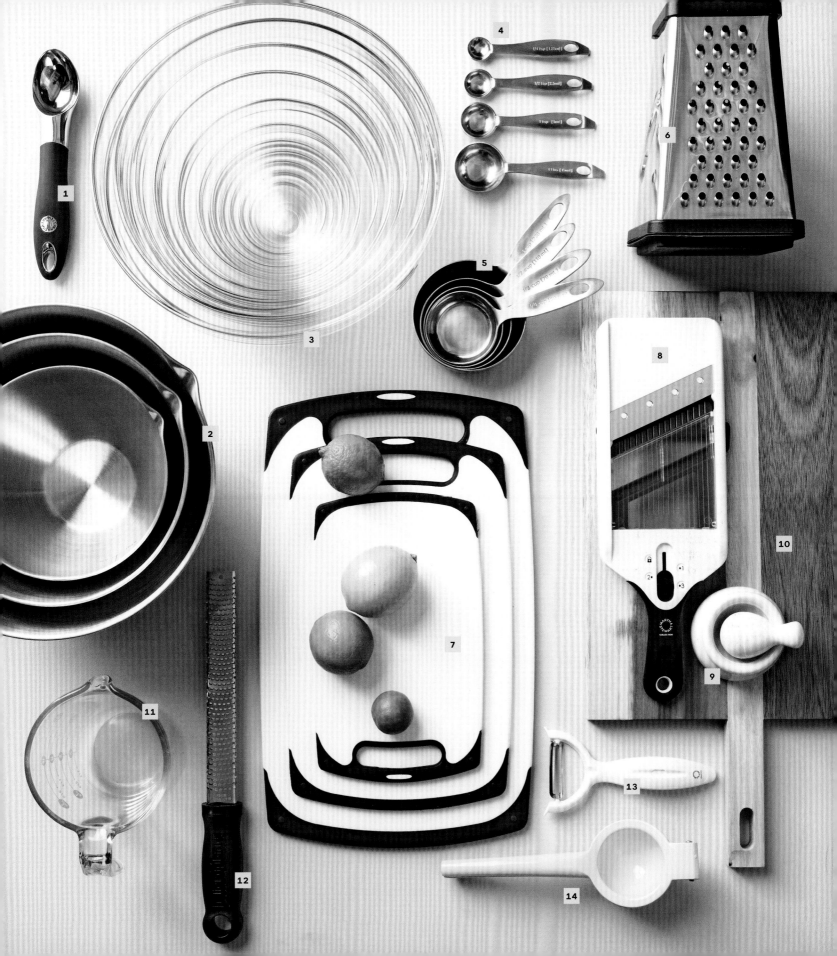

POTS AND PANS

Your cookware choices can seem endless—especially when you're trying to build a collection. Here are the pots and pans we recommend bringing into your kitchen, including the best sizes, shapes, and materials to look for.

1. Stockpot
You'll find a stockpot indispensable in the kitchen, even though it takes up a good bit of room in any cabinet. Here's why it's worth it: You'll reach for it to make soups, stocks, and broths, as well as steamed clams, shellfish, or other seafood. Look for one that's 8 to 10 quarts in size and relatively tall and narrow.

2. Roasting pan and rack
In a pinch you can roast a chicken in a cast-iron skillet, but for all kinds of kitchen tasks, a roasting pan really comes in handy—not only can you roast two chickens, a Thanksgiving turkey, or vegetables, but you can make a big batch of lasagna, macaroni and cheese, or roasted fruit. You can also use it as a water bath when baking custards and cheesecake. Choose a sturdy pan with upright riveted handles that are big enough to grasp securely while wearing oven mitts. Unlike a nonstick coating, a stainless-steel finish allows the pan drippings to brown—the secret to any flavorful gravy or pan sauce. A roasting rack will elevate the food, allowing air to circulate underneath.

3. Large skillet
When it comes to putting meals on the table fast, a 10- or 12-inch skillet is the first thing you should grab. It's just what you need to sauté or stir-fry chicken, seafood, and vegetables ranging from A (asparagus) to Z (zucchini). An ovenproof handle is a big plus—it allows you to sear a steak on the stovetop, then pop the whole thing in the oven to finish cooking.

4. Dutch oven
Like a stockpot, a Dutch oven takes up some room but opens up worlds of possibility in the kitchen: Especially when it comes to entertaining, the wonders of a flavorful (and make-ahead) braise can't be beat. A Dutch oven made of enameled cast iron evenly distributes and retains heat, is attractive enough to move from stove to table, and is a dream to clean.

5. Large saucepan
This is a real kitchen workhorse, one that will practically live on your stovetop, because it's ideal for almost everything— tomato sauce, mashed potatoes, risotto, oatmeal and other grains, steamed vegetables, a small amount of pasta, or one-pot soups and stews. Look for a comfortable, well-balanced handle and a 4-quart size.

6. Cast-iron skillet
Sunny-side up or over easy? Your cast-iron skillet may be the first pan you turn to in the morning for short-order eggs and the one you reach for after a long day to sear a burger or steak. Its surface conducts heat evenly and browns beautifully, so it should be your go-to pan for cornbread and upside-down cake, too. And if you're unsure about how to season cast iron, not to worry; these days, you can find "preseasoned" cast iron—or if you're in the market for an instant heirloom, look for a previously owned, well-seasoned beauty at yard sales or online.

7. Cast-iron grill pan
There's no reason to let a downpour—or the lack of a backyard—stop you when you're craving a cookout: A cast-iron ridged grill pan makes indoor grilling of everything from burgers and hotdogs to steak, fish, and vegetables quick and easy. To get distinctive, delicious-looking grill marks, preheat the pan for 5 to 10 minutes over medium heat or higher.

8. Straight-sided skillet
This fabulous "do-anything" pan turns you into a "do-anything" cook: You can sauté vegetables, cook a mess of greens, make coq au vin, poach salmon, even shallow-fry meatballs. The secret to its versatility? Its straight sides and broad bottom allow plenty of room to brown things well (flipping fish fillets or chicken breast halves is a cinch) or to stir and toss food while cooking. A helper handle on the side makes it easy to move the pan in and out of the oven; the lid, sometimes sold separately, is a smart add-on.

9. Small saucepan
A small saucepan is one of your best friends in the kitchen. You'll rely on it again and again for hard-cooking eggs, making hot cereal, reheating leftovers, stewing fruit, or melting butter.

COOKING EQUIPMENT

Make sure to stock these essentials—and place them within easy reach—so you never find yourselves mid-recipe, stranded at the stove, without a spoon or strainer in sight.

1. Spatula

A single tool can flip a burger or a pancake, or gently turn a delicate piece of fish. With its sturdy handle and thin head, a spatula is comfortable to grip and can delicately slide under food to turn it without tearing or crumbling. If you're using a nonstick pan, choose a silicone-coated spatula.

2. Ladle

Serve all manner of soups and stews from an all-purpose ladle—without spilling a drop. Choose a ladle with a curved handle for a party punch; the handle can hook over the edge of the punch-bowl. For gravy and sauces, you'll want a smaller ladle (usually with a handle that's 5 inches or shorter).

3. Slotted spoon

When you want to test vegetables for doneness, separate meat from rendered fat, or skim foam from a simmering pot of beans, you want a slotted spoon for the job. In addition to using it to separate ingredients from liquids during cooking, it's an ideal serving spoon for vegetables, fruit, or meat that's cooked in broth or gravy.

4. Large spoon

Sometimes cooking seems like one big adventure in stirring. A long-handled cooking spoon will be there for you, and, as with this stainless-steel version, be handsome enough to go right to the table when it's time to eat.

5. Baking spatulas

Mix, fold, stir, scrape. A spatula is a brownie- and cake-baker's best friend. Look for one made with silicone, which is heat-resistant, less breakable than rubber, and flexible enough to scrape every last drop of batter from a mixing bowl (or reach every dollop of mayonnaise or peanut butter from a jar).

6. Thermometer

When it comes to determining the doneness of meats, from a roasted Thanksgiving turkey to weeknight pork chops, temperature is key. An instant-read thermometer will take away any guesswork. Classic models are straightforward, require no batteries, and have an easy-to-read dial. Digital models require batteries and cost a bit more, but are more accurate to the degree.

7. Spider

No, it has nothing to do with a daddy longlegs, but it *is* weblike. This spider has a long handle and a wide, fine-mesh basket that keeps your hands well clear of boiling water or sizzling oil and allows you to easily scoop out pasta, dumplings, or French fries.

8. Tongs

Anyone who's ever tried to turn vegetables on a grill without tongs knows that sinking feeling when the rounds of zucchini begin to slip through the grill grates. Long-handled tongs provide the firm grip you need (and distance from the heat) to grab those vegetables, char peppers over a gas flame, snag an ear of corn from boiling water or a piece of beef from a braising liquid, or turn baked potatoes in the oven.

9. Wooden spoon

The wooden spoon may be the tool cooks reach for before any other. Good-looking, inexpensive, available in a number of sizes and shapes, and cool under fire (they don't conduct heat like metal tools), they'll stir everything from sauces to stir-fries to cookie dough. Wood does absorb flavors, though, so keep one spoon for savory foods and another for sweet ones.

10. Whisk

Omelets are built on eggs whisked to a light froth, and you'll need this tool for a proper meringue or whipped cream. Flexible wires (often in a balloon shape, as pictured, and coated with silicone to protect nonstick pans) help whip ingredients lightly. This is your go-to tool for pan sauces and vinaigrettes and for "sifting" dry ingredients when baking.

11. Colander

Washing fruits and vegetables before eating them raw or cooking them is nonnegotiable for food safety. There's no better tool than the colander for washing and draining. If you're a pasta-with-vegetables fan, you may claim it as one of your most-used tools. Look for sturdy handles and holes that are small enough so that ultrathin pasta won't escape.

12. Potato masher

A potato masher does much more than give you perfectly smashed spuds: It can help you make a batch of guacamole in a heartbeat and break up ground beef in a skillet just as quickly. Even if mashed potatoes aren't a regular side for you, smashed cauliflower might be. The silicone masher pictured has a flip head, so that it can be stored flat in a drawer when your work is done.

BAKING TOOLS

Not everyone's a born baker, but anyone can learn—and keeping the right equipment on hand opens you up to a world of possibilities. This may be a starter set, but it can take you way beyond the basics.

1. Muffin tin
Blueberry, corn, lemon–poppy seed, bran—everybody has a favorite muffin, and, along with cupcakes, they're among the quickest things to bake. With a standard (12-cup) tin handy, they're just the beginning; you can use the pan for popovers, individual meatloaves, and little quiches.

2. Cooling rack
Every kitchen should have a wire rack: It lets air circulate under a cooling cake so it stays perfect, and prevents baked cookies or cake layers from getting soggy. Set in a rimmed baking sheet, it's also just right for keeping waffles or pancakes warm while making another batch, or catching glazes as they are drizzled over cakes and cookies.

3. Round cake pan
Just the sight of a homemade layer cake can bring down the house. And although a layer cake isn't hard to make, it helps to have a pair of straight-sided pans that will yield even, easy-to-frost layers; they also work well for cinnamon buns and even deep-dish pizza. Layer cake recipes usually call for two 9-inch pans.

4. Square cake pan
Homey treats like brownies, gingerbread, and bar cookies are a breeze to make when you have a square pan at the ready.

5. Offset baking spatula
Think of this long, narrow spatula as an extension of your hand. Its angled handle lifts your grip, so you can evenly spread a batter into every corner of the pan, and the pliable, rounded blade makes quick, easy work of swirling and swooping frosting. It's strong and long enough to transfer a cake layer from cooling rack to cake plate, and you can also use it to separate a baked tart from the bottom of the pan or remove cookies from a baking sheet.

6. Loaf pan
Pound cake, quick breads, and meatloaf are all rich and delicious—they're also simple to pull together and any leftovers (if you should be so lucky) keep beautifully. Having a loaf pan or two on hand makes it easy to work them into your regular kitchen routine.

7. Rectangular baking dish
This shape is ideal for baking fruit crisps and cobblers, as well as layered dishes like lasagna and scalloped potatoes—its broad surface area encourages the evaporation of liquid, and a depth of about 2 inches promotes even cooking.

8. Bench scraper
Like an offset spatula (see above), this handy tool is an extension of your hand: Sweep chopped ingredients from a cutting board into a bowl, scrape trimmings into the compost pail, loosen dough from a work surface, divide dough into neat, even portions—you'll find a different use for it every time you pick it up.

9. Pastry blender
Tender, flaky, crisp: Delicious pastry is all about the texture you get when you keep the dough moving quickly. And when it comes to a seize-the-moment batch of biscuits or seasonal fruit pie, your secret weapon is something your great-grandmother would recognize: a pastry blender. Just push the fat (usually cubed chilled butter) through the flour while rotating the U-shaped wires a quarter turn, so they cut and blend quickly and simultaneously.

10. Rolling pin
No handles, no brakes! Rolling out dough into a circle or other shape is as easy as pie when you use a French-style rolling pin—a sleek, handle-less cylinder that may or may not be tapered. It's lighter and more maneuverable than the two-handled American type.

11. Pastry brush
This tool may be small, but it never fails to deliver a drip-free, even coating. Use it to brush egg wash on a pie crust, glaze the fruit on top of a tart, or saturate cake layers with a flavored syrup or liqueur.

12. Rimmed baking sheet
This is one versatile go-to pan: It's perfect for baking bar cookies and toasting croutons, breadcrumbs, nuts, or granola. When it comes to sweets, it's the pan of choice for a rolled sheet cake (think Swiss roll), and it'll also work for biscuits and buns.

13. Cookie sheet
If you love to make cookies, then this is the baking sheet of your dreams; the small lip at one end for handling makes it easy to slide cookies onto a cooling rack (and the flat sides allow air to circulate). Buy two, so you can bake two dozen at once; or, alternately, one sheet can cool while the other is in the oven.

14. Silicone spatula
How did we ever live without smartphones, ATMs—and silicone spatulas? One great advantage is that the material can be used on any cooking surface, including delicate nonstick; look for a spatula that's heatproof and tapered, so it slips under food easily.

15. Pie plate
A 9-inch ceramic pie plate is pretty enough to be brought to the table for serving, but it has a practical side as well: It heats evenly, helping to produce a nicely browned crust. You can also use it for quiches and other savory pies.

SERVING ESSENTIALS

When you merge your kitchens, take stock of what you each already have: You'll probably end up doubling, even tripling, up on certain items (the more serving platters, the merrier!) and replacing others with better-quality versions (go ahead and ditch those plastic cereal bowls for a set of hand-thrown ceramic ones). Make sure you have the basics for everyday meals—at least eight each of dinner plates, salad plates, bowls, and so on (to account for the rotation from table to dishwasher to cabinet). You can always fill in the gaps by registering for any missing pieces or buying them yourselves.

Of course, there will be times when you want to trot out a fancy new recipe, pop open a bottle of your finest red, and invite friends over—and you'll need to be prepared. When you're asking guests to share a home-cooked meal, after all, you're committing to more than just feeding them. You're treating them to a social gathering centered around food that's a bit more thoughtful—or at least more plentiful—than your normal weeknight fare. Having the right entertaining pieces at your disposal—beautiful table linens, stylish stemware, and serving pieces—is an easy way to telegraph that "something special."

Following are some guidelines designed to help you narrow your options when it comes to choosing (and editing out) dinnerware, glassware, serveware, linens, and tabletop accessories that will work for you—for the long haul.

Dinnerware

If you're the type who started coveting a certain china pattern as soon as you got engaged (or even earlier), congratulations! You know what you want; now go forth and get it, even if you have to build your collection slowly, piece by piece. But if you're like the majority of the newly engaged or newly wed, you're overwhelmed by the dizzying array of dinnerware choices out there. For those undecideds, think white.

You simply cannot go wrong with a set of white dinnerware. Why? First, the color works for both everyday and special-occasion meals. Second, you can always add pattern and color via table linens, which can be easily updated as the seasons—and your tastes—change; buying a whole new dinnerware set, on the other hand, is a bigger investment. Third, white is classic; it should never feel so-ten-years-ago. And last, as food photographers everywhere will tell you, your culinary creations just look more enticing presented on an unadorned white plate.

As for flatware, consider registering for a set of gold-plated forks, spoons, and knives in addition to your everyday set if you have the storage space. They automatically elevate any dining table, add a festive sparkle to your settings, and are available at wildly different price points.

You should also invest in some small plates. Salad, bread, dessert, and appetizer plates are all sized smaller than dinner plates. No need to collect every size: Generally, as long as you have enough plates for hors d'oeuvres and dessert courses, you have enough to entertain.

Charger plates, on the other hand, may be a must-have at four-star restaurants, but in your home, they're an only-if-you-want-to (or if you happen to have inherited some that you love).

Glassware

Even if you and your partner aren't wine drinkers, bottles of vino will likely show up uninvited—it is, after all, one of the most popular hostess gifts—and you'll want to be prepared to serve it. If you're a true oenophile, consider collecting a range of glasses that allow for the fullest appreciation of a variety of wines (glasses made specifically, for instance, for Bordeaux, Pinot Noir, or Chardonnay). But if you don't have the super-sensitive olfactory and taste receptors of a sommelier—which is to say, if you're like most people—you should be fine with just two glass types: one for white and one for red.

You could even go with just one wine glass for reds *and* whites; simply pick one designated as "all-purpose" or choose your favorite shape. Chances are no one's going to complain about sipping Sauvignon Blanc from a Merlot

glass. And if you're really into unfussy, streamlined entertaining, consider stemless wine glasses, which are great for casual get-togethers and can double as tumblers for other drinks, from lemonade to whiskey sours.

Also consider adding champagne flutes to your shelves. They're certainly not a necessity, but they do help bubblies stay fizzy and add presence to any toast.

After you've figured out your wine glass collection, think about your other bar needs. What's your favorite drink when you want to unwind? Whatever it is, make sure to stock up on the corresponding vessel, whether it's an old-fashioned tumbler, brandy snifter, sake cup, or pilsner glass.

Keep small juice glasses in mind as well. While there's no scientific evidence to confirm this, many swear that drinks simply taste better when poured into a nice little glass from a glass pitcher (choose one of those, too!). If you like to have people over for brunch or just linger with your partner over the Sunday paper, you'll definitely want to stock up on these.

A wine decanter, however, is not essential. It's a nice touch to pour a bottle into a pretty decanter and allow it to aerate—but totally unnecessary for the average wine drinker.

Serveware

To figure out what type of serveware you'll need, think about what type of food you like to serve. If you always offer a salad, you'll want to make sure you have a big salad bowl and a pretty pair of servers. If pasta is often on the menu, put big, family-style bowls on your list. And if your specialty happens to be customized pizzas, you'll want to pick up a pizza stone and peel. These large items can take up valuable cabinet space, so purchase them only if you'll use them with some frequency.

There are some serving pieces, however, that every host should own, no matter the cooking style: a tried-and-true board to display a selection of cheeses, but also to hold other nibbles like olives, fruit, and nuts; a butter dish; a bread basket; a gravy boat, which may be used just once a year, but is still important if you host Thanksgiving; some trays; and, last but not least, a serving platter—or ten. You can present virtually any type of food on a platter—whole salmon, a selection of cured meats, colorful vegetables hot off the grill, and so on.

A cake stand is definitely worth having. Displaying a birthday cake, even a store-bought one, on a stand makes the occasion feel that much more special. Besides, it's not just for cake. It can be deployed to present almost any dessert beautifully.

You probably don't need a chips-and-dip platter. It's certainly handy, but you can easily mimic one by putting a small bowl or a ramekin in the middle of a more attractive multipurpose platter.

Linens

Just as tablecloths at a restaurant are shorthand for "fancy," a covered dining table in your home denotes "special occasion." If you've decided that white dinnerware is for you, then you might want to start amassing tablecloths or runners in whatever colors or patterns—whether bright florals or muted neutral solids or bold stripes—speak to you. Choose napkins to coordinate with them, but avoid anything too matchy-matchy, which can feel old-fashioned. For instance, if your tablecloth features a pattern, refrain from grabbing matching napkins; instead choose ones in the same (or a nicely contrasting) color palette.

You can always opt for fail-safe white table linens for some of the same reasons that white dinnerware works so well (namely, that they're timeless). In addition, white linens can be bleached, which means most food stains can usually be erased.

As for place mats, they're not only functional, protecting the tablecloth from drips and drops, they're also another opportunity to add pattern or texture to your tablescape.

You can probably forgo napkin rings, however. By all means, purchase them if you see yourself using them, but you can certainly set a memorable (even formal) table without them.

Entertaining Accessories

You now have what you need to serve the food and your guests will have what they need to enjoy it. What's missing? Little touches that enhance an appreciation of the meal and the company. With that in mind, make sure to procure vases and candleholders, in a few sizes and heights, for your dining room (flowers provide natural beauty and candlelight gives off a warm, flattering glow).

Instead of salt and pepper shakers on the table, try freshly ground pepper and flaky sea salt, set in stylish salt and pepper cellars. This seemingly small detail will help to elevate your guests' experiences.

On the other hand, place-card holders can seem unnecessarily fussy. If you prefer assigned seating at your table, simply position place cards directly on the plates—or get creative and make your own holders!

ORDER IN THE KITCHEN

For better or for worse, there's no single right way to organize a kitchen: Your kitchen could be tiny or huge, you could be combining your gear or starting from scratch—no matter what, a well-ordered space makes spending time there easier. Find a system that works best for the two of you; it will affect not just how and what you cook, but how you plan meals and even shop. If your cabinets are hugely cluttered, it's hard to tell whether you need to buy a can of tomatoes, or even where to look. If this is a recurring problem in your kitchen, it's time to get things in order before they get out of hand. Here are a few suggestions:

1. GROUP LIKE WITH LIKE.

Look for pots and pans that can be nestled together for storage or those that display well together on a pot rack; use a slotted rack on the inside of a cabinet door for lids. Similarly, buy one good-quality set of food-storage containers in graduated sizes that nest or stack neatly; store them with reusable water bottles and other on-the-go gear.

Keep wooden spoons in the same stove-side crock, all the bakeware in the same cupboard, and all the barware and cocktail glasses together. Group dinnerware and glassware so the plates, bowls, cups, and glasses you use every day all live in one convenient place.

If you have an overflow of serving pieces in the same color or pattern, or from the same era, look for interesting opportunities to display them, especially if you're low on cabinet space. Grouping them on top of the cupboards or on the bottom shelf of the island can help a random assortment look like a curated collection—as long as it doesn't look like a hodgepodge. Keep palette, scale, and time period in mind.

2. STORE IT WHERE YOU USE IT.

Storing things close to where you use them means saved steps and saved time, and is one secret to harmony in the kitchen. It's all too easy to find yourselves working at cross purposes (and exchanging cross words) when one person is emptying the dishwasher and the other is focused on dinner prep. Store plates, glasses, and flatware near the dishwasher for easy unloading, and place everyday cooking tools (whisks, wooden spoons, tongs) and ingredients (salt, pepper, olive oil) close to the stove. Store cutting boards upright to conserve space, and place them near the countertop where you chop, slice, and dice, along with knives and a few small prep (*mise en place*) bowls.

3. IF YOU REACH FOR IT OFTEN, KEEP IT CLOSE.

If you need to use a step stool on a daily basis, then something's wrong. Instead, place everyday essentials within easy reach; that means commonly used pantry items are stored at eye level and

things that require heavy lifting—a Dutch oven, a large cast-iron skillet, or stand mixer, for example—below waist level. There's no reason to keep rarely used items (say, a turkey platter or an ice cream maker) in the kitchen at all. Wrap them up (to keep them clean), then stash them away wherever you have extra space, like in the basement or garage.

4. ASSESS, PURGE, REPEAT.

Think of it this way: Yard sales and secondhand stores exist for a reason. Do an initial purge once you get married, and then again once a year. Pretend you are moving, and take inventory of your pots and pans, tools, utensils, and dishes. Get rid of anything you don't use regularly. Be ruthless: How many of those slotted spoons do you actually need? And if that basement shelf doesn't have room for the panini press, maybe that's a sign that neither do you.

5. CONTAIN YOURSELF.

This can be as simple as using trays or rimmed baking sheets to corral groups of things—like the sugar, honey,

and spoons you keep next to the tea, or the seasonings and olive oil by the stovetop; a tray will help catch drips, speed cleanup, and make it easy to move everything out of the way when you need to. Or it can be as elaborate as transferring things from the original packaging into matching containers. This definitely makes your shelves look more tidy and orderly, and can immediately help you keep calm when you walk into the kitchen. Choose whichever method of containment matches your style, personality, and most pressing need.

You may also want to subdivide the space in drawers and cabinets to keep small items neat and easy to find; group napkins and kitchen towels together; likewise, utensils and knives; and corral the stuff that you don't know what else to do with into a designated "junk" drawer: rubber bands, pencils, twine, batteries, glue, a ruler, a permanent marker, and so on. Remember to assess and purge the junk drawer every month or so.

COUNTER INTELLIGENCE

The countertop is the key to any functioning kitchen. After all, it's where you do most of the work, whether it's making sandwiches, chopping vegetables and herbs, cutting up a whole chicken, or rolling out pie dough. That's why it makes sense to keep your biggest stretch of countertop clear of clutter and small appliances. You'll be thrilled at how easy this makes it to cook anything your heart desires. (And don't worry if there isn't a lot of counter space in your current kitchen; there are ways to work around that.)

1. CREATE STATIONS FOR EVERY DAY.

Turn the space next to a wall outlet into your go-to breakfast spot, grouping a coffeemaker, toaster, and whatever else you need to start the day there. If juices or smoothies are part of your morning routine, that's where the juicer or blender should live, too. A shelf or open cabinet over this section of the counter makes a good home for a bread box, glass jars filled with cereals and granola, an airtight container of coffee beans or tea, mugs, and spoons. Just add milk, and your day is off to a great start!

Because heat and light are detrimental to olive oil—any cooking oil, really—store it in a small bottle that you can refill as needed, and keep your main supply somewhere cool, dark, and dry.

Beside the sink, use one little tray or dish for sponges and another for hand and dish soaps. It takes no time to decant dish soap from a large plastic bottle into a smaller, more streamlined container. And it makes dishwashing seem like less of a chore if the area around the sink looks neat and tidy.

2. EDIT OUT THE UNNECESSARY.

If you can go for days (or weeks) on end without using a blender, food processor, stand mixer, rice cooker, or other small appliance, tuck it away in a drawer, cupboard, or lower shelf. The same goes for pantry items such as sugar, flour, and oatmeal.

For times when you only have a few things to wash, instead of dedicating counter space to an unwieldy dish-drying rack, simply place a wire rack into a rimmed sheet pan and let those two tools work double duty. After the dishes are dry, the rack and pan can go right back into a cabinet or drawer.

And if you have the drawer space, outfit one of them with a slotted bamboo knife box so you don't need to keep a bulky knife block on the counter.

3. PUT WALL SPACE TO USE.

A row of hooks or a pegboard mounted on the wall over the counter offers easy access to graters, peelers, corkscrews, and other small miscellaneous tools that are often jumbled in a drawer; they can support small wire baskets for garlic or shallots, too.

A simple board-and-bracket shelf in an otherwise cramped or underutilized corner keeps things off the counter. Thin shelves give you extra storage space for bulk spices or coffee mugs without feeling heavy or imposing, even in a cramped spot. A wider, sturdier shelf mounted over a doorway or window makes room for extra plates and bowls for entertaining.

A paper-towel holder mounted in a cabinet leaves more room on the counter than a standing one.

A slim (yet sturdy) metal towel bar built into a well-anchored shelf or attached to the wall can be outfitted with S hooks for hanging pots and pans. If space is tight, intersperse pots of different sizes instead of arranging them in graduating order.

When it comes to wall space, everything is fair game, including the sides of your cabinet or refrigerator. Install a row of cup hooks along the edge of your countertop or island for kitchen towels, or store your most frequently used spices in magnetized containers on the side of the fridge.

4. ILLUMINATE YOUR WORK SURFACE.

Even if your kitchen has a wealth of windows that let the sun pour in, countertops are often hidden in shadows. Under-cabinet or under-shelf lighting brightens those areas, and the options are many, including LED strips, tape lighting, and updated fluorescent strips. One easy solution: Install so-called puck lighting (the individual little hockey-puck-shaped lights), which don't require hardwiring. They can be plugged in or even run on batteries.

5. ADD COUNTER SPACE WITHOUT COUNTERS.

If, even after decluttering, you're still left with very little counter space, create some: An over-the-sink cutting board or integrated sink cutting board lets the area pull double duty—and an aluminum or stainless steel stovetop cover is another multitasker. If you have room in the kitchen, a worktable cart or mobile kitchen island, with or without a butcher-block top, gives you movable work space.

STORAGE EFFICIENCY

It's not the amount of room you have that matters but how you manage it. Even if you can't renovate the kitchen or add more cabinets or drawers, you can easily improve upon what's there. And maximizing your storage makes any kitchen feel more open because it automatically cuts down on clutter. Whatever your kitchen type, you can create beautiful, efficient, perfect-for-your-storage-needs space.

When your square footage is tiny, try this easy fix: Remove the doors from the upper cabinets and paint the inside to complement the walls. The space instantly feels bigger, and keeping things on display is a great incentive to pare down to the essentials. You're also bound to use things more if you can see them. On the flip side, tuck things that you don't need all the time in labeled matching baskets or boxes, and store them on top of the cabinets. If, after a while, you can't remember the last time you reached for that basket or box, then it's time to toss out whatever's in there, or move it to longer-term storage.

1. ADD EASY ACCESS. Revolving trays, also known as lazy Susans, are a good bet for organizing spices or condiments so you can quickly find what you need. Instead of wasting cabinet space on a single layer of drinking glasses or canned goods, consider expandable wire risers; they instantly double the available space. Pull-out shelves or risers keep canned and boxed goods from getting lost in the back of the cabinet.

2. GROUP ACCORDING TO FLAVORS AND USES. Organize sauces, oils, and vinegars by cuisine, and do the same for open condiments in the refrigerator. That way, you can quickly and easily put a stir-fry on the table one night and enjoy taco night the next. This goes for breakfast ingredients (syrups, dried fruits, jams, and preserves), baking supplies (flours, sugars, baking powder and soda), pastas, whole grains, dried beans, and so on. If you have multiples of one item—strawberry jam or tomato sauce, for instance—rotate your stock when you put things away on the shelves, so that you use the oldest products first.

3. DECANT AND CONTAINERIZE. Decant whole grains, dried beans, and other bulk items into airtight glass jars or other see-through containers. You're more likely to use things if they're more visible, plus buying in bulk is less expensive and less wasteful when it comes to packaging. You may even find yourself saving glass jars to decant and/or organize all sorts of foods—rice, nuts, popcorn, pasta, cereal, crackers, pretzels, cookies, even dog treats. Jars keep things fresh, look attractive on the shelf, and enable you to see what you have at a glance. Adding a label to each container makes life even easier.

4. SNEAK IN STORAGE WHEREVER YOU CAN. The insides and outsides of cabinets are valuable real estate: The inside of a door, for example, can hold magnetic strips for small tins of finishing salts or spices, or you could line it with corkboard to organize lists and recipes—or even photos. Hang rubber gloves or cleaning cloths from hooks on the inside of the door under the sink. You can also install pegboard or magnetic strips in the space between your countertop and cabinets to hold knives and small metal tools.

REFRIGERATOR MANAGEMENT

The refrigerator is the cook's best friend. Use it wisely, and not only will you always have the makings for supper—even if it's stir-fried leftovers or bacon and eggs—but you'll save money by preventing energy and food waste as well. Today's refrigerators are high-tech appliances that allow you to store many different types of foods under optimal conditions. Think of the separate shelves and compartments as neighborhoods or microclimates. The lower shelves are the chilliest (because cold air sinks), for instance, and so that's where you should keep raw meat, seafood, dairy, and eggs. Crisper drawers maintain high humidity, perfect for preserving the shelf life of fresh produce; reserve the door—the warmest part of the refrigerator—for condiments, juices, and other foods that don't spoil easily.

1. BE ENERGY-EFFICIENT.

Avoid overstuffing the refrigerator; air needs to circulate in order to keep food at an even temperature. The freezer, however, works at peak efficiency when packed full—a good reason to make big batches of soup or chili, or store cold packs for picnics or road trips.

A too-cold temperature in the refrigerator wastes energy and can even freeze (and thereby ruin) delicate foods like lettuce. It should be set at or below 40°F; the freezer temperature should be kept at 0°F.

Your refrigerator's condenser coils can't work well if they're coated with grime or dust, so twice a year, unplug the fridge and use a coil brush or the crevice attachment on a vacuum cleaner to clean the coils. Do this more often if your refrigerator has the coils on top or if you have pets.

2. MAXIMIZE SHELF SPACE.

Using square or rectangular stackable containers rather than round ones enables you to store more food and keep things neater. An assortment of small stackables means that you can easily pack leftovers for grab-and-go lunches. If space is at a premium, don't let unopened cans of soda or single-serve bottles of water muscle out food that needs to be kept cold. Instead, store shelf-stable bottles and cans in the pantry, and chill them with ice cubes.

3. KEEP IT WHERE YOU CAN SEE IT.

Whoever first coined the phrase "When in doubt, throw it out" must have been peering into a refrigerator. We've all been there—discovering a week-old basket of strawberries at the back of a shelf, or a half-full carton of sour cream that looks like a science experiment. The problem pretty much solves itself if you keep highly perishable items right where you can see them. Tender herbs fall into this category: Fresh basil makes a tasty caprese sandwich—much better than finding a past-its-prime bundle in a forgotten corner of the fridge.

Finally, keeping small containers of cut-up fruits and vegetables or hard-cooked eggs at eye level makes it easy to do the right thing when it comes to snacks.

4. CLEAN AS YOU GO.

A thorough cleaning of the refrigerator twice a year isn't nearly as onerous with a few preemptive practices. Line crisper bins with paper towels, and keep sticky jars of preserves or syrup in removable shelf bins, which are easy to rinse and replace.

To avoid leaks from packages of meat or poultry, get in the habit of double-bagging and storing them on a plate, or packing them in an airtight container on the bottom shelf—your dedicated "meat locker" section.

Change the filter for your water dispenser every six months. A clogged filter is often the culprit for slow drips and super-small ice cubes.

5. MAKE YOUR FREEZER WORK FOR YOU.

With a strategically stocked freezer, you'll never be at a loss for a good meal again. In addition to the usual suspects like broths, sauces, soups, stews, meats, and vegetables, you can freeze bread, tortillas, milk, hard cheeses, chopped herbs, cooked beans (which can go straight from the freezer into a soup pot), casseroles, pizza dough, and even whole baked pies. Two must-haves for the home cook are freezer-safe glass containers and freezer-safe resealable plastic bags (freeze their contents flat, then, when frozen solid, stack them sideways). Keep everything labeled with the contents and date, and do a regular sweep to see what you might work into your weekly dinner rotation and to toss out anything that is past its prime.

PANTRY BASICS

The following list is a guide to many of the items we use in the test kitchen at Martha Stewart Living. Because we think of them as building blocks of flavor, they go beyond single uses and inspire us to improvise and create delicious food every day. They also reflect the time crunch we all face (canned beans for weeknight pastas; dried beans for a weekend stew), as well as the health and sustainability issues on everyone's radar. A selection of oils, for example, gives us alternatives to the heavier saturated fats found in butter and cream. And it's never been easier to find meat, eggs, and milk from farmers' markets and other local sources. You'll also discover everything you need to put together protein-rich meatless meals. Even with just a few of these ingredients in your pantry, you should have the makings of dozens of tasty breakfasts, lunches, and dinners.

THE ESSENTIALS

Beans and other legumes (dried and canned)

Black beans, chickpeas, and white beans (navy, Great Northern, or cannellini) are all versatile: Add them to salads, soups, stews, or pasta dishes. You'll get the most bang for your buck with dried beans, though you do have to plan ahead (they must be soaked before using). Cook up a big batch, and freeze what you don't use. Lentils cook the quickest—no soaking required. You can't go wrong with common brown lentils, but if you see small green French lentils, pounce. Their flavor is more delicate and they hold their shape better. Canned beans are one of the world's great convenience foods, but rinse and drain them well before using to remove much of the salt.

Canned broth

Having chicken and vegetable broth on hand allows you to fast-track a soup or stew. Add a splash or two to vegetables as they cook to amp up the taste or moisten leftovers when reheating. Always use low-sodium broths, and choose organic whenever possible. **PANTRY TIP:** If you buy broth in cartons rather than cans, it can be refrigerated once opened for up to two weeks or so; mark the date you opened it on the carton.

Canned coconut milk

The creamy, mild sweetness of unsweetened coconut milk, made from pressed fresh coconut meat, balances the hot, pungent flavors in many Southeast Asian or Caribbean soups, stews, curries, and rice dishes. Having a can at the ready, along with Thai green chile paste and dried Asian noodles, will save you from ordering takeout too often.

Canned tomatoes

You can count on canned tomatoes to be consistent, inexpensive, widely available, and much more flavorful than fresh tomatoes out of season. Whole tomatoes in juice (not puree) are your best all-around bet: Add them to soups, stews, braised meat dishes, chilis, and more. They can be crushed with your hands for use in quick-cooking sauces, pureed until smooth as an alternative to jarred sauces, or slow-roasted to add to sandwiches, salads, and omelets—even as a side to grilled steak. **PANTRY TIP:** Eliminate the juicy mess of chopping canned tomatoes: Use kitchen shears to chop them while they're still in the can.

Dried pastas

Among the dizzying displays of dried pastas at any supermarket are countless shapes and sizes, including gluten-free alternatives. Spaghetti and spaghettini work well for all types of sauces, as does thicker bucatini (sometimes called perciatelli), which is basically fat, hollow spaghetti. Penne gets along with most sauces, too; the hollow tubes (especially the ridged ones, called rigate) trap flavorful sauces, as do twisted shapes like fusilli or campanelle. No-boil lasagna noodles are thin and tender; break any leftover uncooked noodles into pieces and add to soups.

A supply of Asian noodles will serve you well: Flat, wide rice stick noodles for Thai and other Southeast Asian recipes; chewy, bean thread noodles (also called cellophane or glass noodles) for salads and soups (they absorb broths easily); curlicues of instant ramen (skip the additive-laden packet and add your own seasonings, meat, and vegetables); or soba noodles—delicious in soups or served cold with a dipping sauce.

Grains

Whole grains are good for you, delicious, and satisfying. Get in the habit of including bulgur, farro, quick-cooking polenta, and quinoa in weeknight dinners. A big batch of slow-cooking varieties like barley, Kamut, or wheat berries can be made ahead on a weekend and refrigerated or frozen (you can add them directly from the freezer to a soup or stew; no need to thaw). Having big batches also makes it easy and efficient to pack healthier and cheaper alternatives for lunch.

There's a number of oat options to choose from, including old-fashioned rolled oats, which are flattened into flakes and cook in about five minutes, and steel-cut oats—whole grains that are cut crosswise into a few pieces. Those take the longest to cook, but you'll be rewarded with deep, nutty flavor and a chewy texture. Oats aren't the only breakfast grain, of course; you can easily swap them out for barley or brown rice, for example. It's amazing how interchangeable grains are, depending on what you pair them with. Keep a variety on hand and don't hesitate to experiment. **PANTRY TIP:** Decanting grains into airtight glass jars makes them easy to see and use; tape cooking instructions to the jar lid.

Rice is a grain, too— botanically speaking, it's the seeds of a grass plant. When the tough, inedible husk is removed, it reveals brown rice— or red or black rice, depending on the color of the nutritious bran layer. They are all 100 percent whole grain; white rice has been milled to remove the bran. Stocking a variety of rices opens the door to some of the world's best dishes.

Couscous is *not* a grain (it's a granular form of pasta), but it's served like one, and since it only takes about five minutes to prepare, it's a quick side-dish option. Israeli couscous (sometimes labeled pearl pasta) is larger, rounder, and heartier.

Mayonnaise

It's hard to imagine sandwiches, potato salad, deviled eggs, and lobster rolls without mayonnaise. Plus, it's an ingenious way to carry flavor—try adding toasted fennel seeds or citrusy coriander seeds to mayo and spreading it over fish before broiling (it also helps keep the fish tender as it cooks). Or spike it with fresh dill or tarragon and serve it on the side. Add a little curry powder and dollop it on steamed asparagus or green beans, or stir in pureed chipotles or smoked paprika and slather it on grilled corn on the cob, Mexican-style.

Oils

Extra-virgin olive oils range in flavor from mild to robust, fruity to peppery. Where to start? Choose an inexpensive one for cooking and something more distinctive to drizzle over salads, pizzas, and pastas. You'll also want a neutral vegetable oil like safflower for mild salad dressings— and for frying, due to its high smoke point. Extra-virgin coconut oil, which comes in a solid state (it turns liquid when heated) has a subtle nutty flavor. It's long been an ingredient in Southeast Asian, Caribbean, and Indian dishes, and is becoming increasingly popular in the United States as a vegan alternative to butter. Try using it for roasting root vegetables and sautéing fish fillets or shrimp. Keep in

mind, though, that coconut oil is higher in saturated fat than olive or canola oil. Heat, light, and time are enemies of all oils, so store them in a dark, cool place and use within a year. **PANTRY TIP:** If you buy olive oil in bulk— at a big-box store, for instance—decant some into a smaller container; store the rest in the pantry.

Panko

These Japanese-style breadcrumbs are made from a loaf that's been dried, then grated, to create a fluffy, flaky, crisp texture. They stay crunchy longer than regular breadcrumbs because they absorb less oil. Use them to coat chicken and fish, and to top gratins and casseroles (including mac and cheese).

Tinned fish

For a quick boost of protein in a salad, late-night sandwiches, or a snack with crackers, nothing beats canned tuna. It's also a good partner for pasta—add sautéed summer vegetables, or white beans, lemon zest, and capers. For the best flavor, look for tuna packed in olive oil; for sustainability, buy pole-caught tuna that's been certified by the Marine Stewardship Council. Wild-caught salmon from Alaska is particularly high in omega-3 fatty acids; sockeye ("red salmon") is heartier in flavor than pink salmon. Cured anchovy fillets add depth to everything from vinaigrettes to tomato sauce. Sardines packed in olive oil are another option for snacks,

salads, and pasta dishes; those that are hand-cut and hand-packed are the most pristine (check the label).

Vinegars

Red-wine and white-wine vinegars—essential in vinaigrettes and marinades, and great last-minute additions to sauces and stews—are kitchen standbys. The sweet intensity of balsamic vinegar means a little goes a long way in vinaigrettes or pan sauces—or simply drizzled over a bowl of ripe strawberries. When shopping for balsamic, look for the words *aceto balsamico tradizionale* on the label to make sure it's the real deal. Renowned for its balanced complexity, sherry vinegar works in just about anything; try just a drizzle with oil on salad greens. Fresh tasting and slightly sweet, cider vinegar gives coleslaw its tang; unfiltered varieties tend to be rounder in flavor. Another supermarket find is unseasoned rice vinegar, which many Asian recipes call for; its low acidity works in vinaigrettes and dipping sauce for dumplings. And if you don't have the exact vinegar called for in a recipe, don't stress out! Play around with what you do have, or adjust it to suit your taste. If you know you prefer a gentle vinaigrette, for instance, swap out rice vinegar or sherry vinegar for a wine vinegar. And if you're caught short, fresh lemon juice can add a welcome acidity to just about any dish.

FLAVOR BOOSTERS

Anchovy paste

Yes, it's made from ground anchovies, salt, and oil, but used in small amounts, this concentrated paste can deliver the savory taste called umami. Add a teaspoon or so to vinaigrettes and pasta sauces, such as tomato or garlic and oil, or work it into softened butter to dollop onto grilled steak, lamb chops, or chicken.

Asian chile sauce and paste

By now, everyone should know to keep a bottle of Sriracha on hand. Beyond using the garlicky sweet-spicy chili sauce for rice dishes and soups, try it on scrambled eggs, mixed into mayonnaise for sandwiches, swirled into cornbread batter, or added to a marinade or barbecue sauce. The Korean hot red-pepper paste called *gochujang* is even more complex and addictive; its robust (yet somehow still mellow) wallop is as at home in a pot roast, slow-cooked ribs, or gazpacho as it is in a bowl of bibimbap.

Chipotle peppers

The smoked jalapeños that have been canned in a tangy tomato sauce are fabulous whizzed in a blender, then stirred into mayonnaise or sour cream for a dip, used as a condiment for drizzling over tacos or a bowl of black bean soup, or spread on sandwiches. Swirl a dab into guacamole or the mashed avocado you put on toast. After using part of a can of chipotles in adobo, refrigerate the remainder in an airtight container.

Dijon mustard

A jar of Dijon mustard is a staple no kitchen should be without. It's a secret weapon in vinaigrettes, pan sauces, and so many dishes—you can combine it with yogurt in a marinade for chicken, mix it with softened butter and parsley to make a compound butter, slather it on chicken or lamb to help a breadcrumb coating adhere, and use it in just about any salad dressing.

Fish sauce

Fish sauce is to Southeast Asia what soy sauce is to China and Japan. In other words, it adds the know-it-when-you-taste-it rich, savory depth of umami. Add it to salad dressings, stir-fries, marinades, or sprinkle a few drops on ripe summer tomatoes. You can even substitute it for Worcestershire sauce or anchovy paste in a pinch. Depending on where it's from, fish sauce can be labeled *nuoc mam* (Vietnam) or *nam pla* (Thailand).

Harissa

For great flavor and a touch of heat, stir this Middle Eastern blend of hot chiles, garlic, olive oil, and spices into pasta or pizza sauces, a lamb or beef meatball mix, chicken or fish marinades, or plain yogurt for a dip. You can also substitute harissa for hot sauce in a dish or cocktail (it's delicious in a Bloody Mary).

Salsa

Look for a jar with the fewest number of ingredients on the label. And think beyond the chip. Whisk salsa into eggs for a frittata, cook it with rice for a speedy side—fabulous with roast chicken and warmed canned beans— or puree it into a barbecue sauce for meats.

Salt-packed capers

Tangy, pungent capers are the unopened flower buds of the caper bush. Those packed in sea salt have a fresher, almost floral flavor and aroma compared with those packed in brine. Always rinse and drain salt-packed capers and use them to "niçoise up" potato, tuna, or egg salads, or to elevate deviled eggs, sliced tomatoes, or steamed green beans. You can also toss them with toasted breadcrumbs and pasta, or add them to any vinaigrette.

Soy sauce and tamari

A drop or two (or three) of soy sauce adds savory-salty magic to marinades (especially for beef), vinaigrettes, braises, stir-fries, soups, and stews. Drizzle it over a quick broccoli sauté, or toss almonds in soy sauce and dry-roast them in a low oven for a few hours. Regular soy sauce is sometimes labeled "thin" soy sauce, and you can't go wrong with Kikkoman—it's readily available, consistently well made (never too salty or harsh), and comes in low-sodium and organic versions. Soy sauce is traditionally brewed from soybeans mixed with a grain—most often wheat. Tamari is a gluten-free soy sauce that's more intense in flavor.

Thai green curry paste

If you like red curry but crave more heat, go for a green curry paste, which is also more herbal. Beyond using it in Southeast Asian curries, noodle dishes, and salads, stir some into mayonnaise or sour cream for a sandwich dip, or work it into a marinade for chicken or seafood.

Worcestershire sauce

This aged, fermented blend that includes anchovies, vinegar, cloves, tamarind, and molasses (there are vegan alternatives) is tangy, pungent, and savory all at once. It pairs perfectly with beef, including marinades, pan sauces, meatloaf, burgers, steaks, braises, or stews— you name it. Also try it in dressings, dips, cocktails (like a Bloody Mary or michelada), or deviled eggs.

SEASONINGS AND SWEETENERS

Salt and pepper

Coarse salt is preferred by chefs and many home cooks because its crystals, which are larger than those of table salt, are convenient to pinch, so you can easily (and generously) season a pot of water for pasta, or a chicken before it goes into the oven. Fine-grained table salt, though, is the one you want for baking. A flaky sea salt like Maldon has large, flat crystals (that don't dissolve rapidly) and a distinctive spiky crunch; it's what's called a finishing salt, used for sprinkling on everything from steamed vegetables to a brownie before serving. For the best flavor, buy black peppercorns whole and freshly grind just what you need.

Spices

If you have no other spices in your drawer, keep these six on hand: cumin, coriander, cayenne pepper, red-pepper flakes, bay leaves, and smoked paprika. Used alone or in various combinations, these can make just about anything taste better. A little cumin or smoked paprika plus a bay leaf jazzes up a bean soup, for example; red-pepper flakes add spark to garlicky braised or sautéed greens; and a little cayenne pepper cuts the richness of twice-baked potatoes or mac and cheese. For baking, add allspice, cloves, cinnamon, cream of tartar, nutmeg, and pure vanilla extract to the mix. **PANTRY TIP:** The flavors and aromas of pre-ground spices diminish quickly when exposed to heat and light, so keep them on a cool, dark shelf and replace them once a year.

Sugar

There's more to sugar than the plain white stuff, especially if you love to bake. Brown sugar is a combination of granulated sugar and molasses; light-brown sugar is more delicate in flavor than the dark variety, but they can generally be used interchangeably. Finely ground confectioners' sugar (also called powdered sugar) dissolves very easily in batters and frostings. Granulated sugar is ideal as a table sweetener and all-around cooking ingredient. Turbinado and Demerara sugars are both minimally processed "raw sugars"; their coarse, crunchy golden brown crystals have a mild caramel flavor. Sanding sugar has large crystals; they're sprinkled on baked goods to make them sparkle. **PANTRY TIP:** Humidity can make sugar lumpy, so keep it in airtight containers in a cool, dry spot. Double-wrap brown sugar to keep it moist.

Maple syrup

Breakfast is just the beginning. Drizzle maple syrup over mashed sweet potatoes and whisk it into a glaze for ham or pork, as well as marinades and pan sauces. Instead of the grades, numbers, or "Vermont Fancy" categories formerly used for American and Canadian maple syrups, now there is just one classification, Grade A. It includes four new color and flavor classes: Golden Color and Delicate Taste; Amber Color and Rich Taste; Dark Color and Robust Taste; and Very Dark Color and Strong Taste.

Molasses

Gingerbread and pumpkin pie get a distinctive spicy, caramel flavor from this traditional sweetener. Baked beans, barbecue sauces, and marinades benefit, too. Molasses comes in different grades: Light (sometimes labeled "original") is mild and mellow; robust or "full-flavored" is less sweet but more complex. Black-strap molasses is too bitter and overpowering to use in most recipes.

BAKING SUPPLIES

Baking powder and baking soda

To get a rise from breads, cakes, and biscuits, you need one of these two different leaveners. They aren't interchangeable; depending on the recipe, you may need one or the other—or both. Before buying, check the expiration date; they lose potency over time and should be replaced once a year. **PANTRY TIP:** An open box of baking soda in the refrigerator helps absorb and eliminate any odors (buy one specifically for that reason and don't use it in cooking).

Chocolate

You can whip up a sauce for ice cream, a batch of cookies, or an easy pudding anytime when you have chocolate bars or chips in the pantry. Many brands have the percentage of cacao (cocoa solids) listed on the label; a higher percentage indicates a more intense, less sweet chocolate flavor. **PANTRY TIP:** Don't worry if chocolate develops a grayish-white "bloom" on the surface; it's harmless and can simply be scraped off.

Cocoa powder

Brownies wouldn't be brownies without cocoa powder. Dutch-process cocoa powder is richer, darker, and less bitter than regular (or "natural") unsweetened cocoa powder. If one or the other cocoa powder isn't specified in a recipe, you can generally use them interchangeably.

Cornstarch

Powdery cornstarch, which is gluten-free, is often used instead of flour (it results in a glossy sheen) as a thickener in pie fillings, pastry cream, and puddings, as well as gravies, soups, and sauces.

Flour

Make unbleached all-purpose flour your go-to choice for pie crusts, cookies, biscuits, pancakes, and waffles. If you're an avid baker, you may want a sack of bread flour and/or cake flour, too. Whole-wheat flour includes the fiber-rich bran. You'll also find freshly ground gluten-free flours made from a variety of grains, such as rice, quinoa, and spelt, at many supermarkets as well as farmers' markets and specialty stores.

REFRIGERATOR AND FREEZER

Bacon

Besides being irresistible on its own or tucked into a sandwich, bacon adds a spark to just about anything. Crumble the crisp-cooked stuff over pan-seared fish fillets, clam or corn chowder, or a salad of hearty greens wilted by the hot bacon drippings. Add to cornbread or corn muffin batter. Brush uncooked strips with maple syrup and sprinkle with a little cayenne pepper, then bake until crunchy for a brunch or cocktail nibble. Check out the offerings at a farmers' market or look for a supermarket brand free of added nitrates or nitrites.

Butter

Unsalted butter has the purest flavor, and it allows you to control the salt in a dish, so it's ideal for all types of cooking, especially baking. Treat yourself to European-style butters, such as Kerrygold or Plugra, which have a higher percentage of butterfat and a richer flavor. Or serve it with radishes and flaky sea salt for an hors d'ocuvre.

Eggs

Really fresh eggs are one of life's simplest luxuries, so, when you can, buy them from a farmers' market or farmer whose chickens are allowed to hunt and peck on pasture. Your omelet will thank you. Large eggs are the most common, and the size we use in our recipes. Shell color simply reflects the breed of hen, not the flavor or nutritional value.

Frozen puff pastry

Possibly a party-giver's best friend, frozen puff pastry can be dressed up in seemingly endless sweet or savory ways. Think chicken potpie, apple turnovers, napoleons, palmiers, cheese straws, pigs in a blanket, a fancy pizza, or a fast, foolproof fruit tart.

Lemons

A squeeze of lemon juice or a little freshly grated lemon zest brightens almost anything— seafood, beans, vegetables, salads, or a pan sauce for steaks. A lemon in the cavity of a roast chicken helps it stay moist and infuses it with flavor; lemon wedges anchor kebabs and turn soft and smoky on the grill. And lemon desserts, with their sunny flavor, carry us through the winter and early spring.

Milk

Gone are the days when the only milk choice you had to make was among whole, 1 or 2 percent, and skim. Now there's cow's milk, goat's milk, and plant-based milks vying for attention—a huge plus if you're vegan, lactose intolerant, or have a food allergy. Buying milk that's free of recombinant bovine growth hormone (rBGH) is a good idea, as is grabbing a carton that's USDA-certified organic and/or comes from a small dairy in your region.

Miso

This protein-rich paste, made from fermented soybeans, is a solid (and instant) flavor foundation. Shiro (white) miso is creamy and mildly salty—a lovely gateway miso that's especially good paired with rice vinegar and safflower oil in a salad dressing or tossed with hot cooked vegetables. Aka (red) miso is fermented longer, so it's stronger in flavor; use it to glaze broiled eggplant, or to give depth to a chocolate sauce (pour

½ cup scalding-hot cream over 3½ ounces chopped bittersweet chocolate; let stand a minute, then whisk in miso) that turns scoops of vanilla into an unforgettable dessert. Awase (mixed) miso is a best-of-both-worlds blend of shiro and aka; it works especially well as a glaze for roasted chicken wings (two parts miso to one part honey; brush toward the end of cooking) or added to a buttery pasta sauce.

Pancetta and prosciutto

Pancetta—which, like bacon, comes from the pork belly—is salt-cured but not smoked, and you can use it anytime you want the flavor of ham without any smokiness. Sauté it with brussels sprouts, toss it with pasta and peas, or add it to a quiche. Prosciutto is ham that's been salted and air-cured but not smoked. It's leaner than pancetta, and its flavor is more delicate and complex. For cocktail hour, add ultrathin slices to a cheese platter, or wrap them around melon slices or halved figs.

Parmesan

If you keep only one cheese in your refrigerator, make it Parmesan. Parmesan is a real team player in any dish, somehow amplifying the other flavors without overpowering them. When shopping, spring for the genuine article, which has "Parmigiano-Reggiano" stamped on the rind. Buy a wedge instead of grated cheese, and grate or shave it just before serving. Wrap it in parchment or wax paper,

then plastic wrap, and store it in the crisper drawer of the refrigerator.

Nuts and seeds

Nuts are truly one of the handiest (and most nutritious) snacks around. You can sprinkle peanuts, walnuts, pecans, or slivered almonds on salads or over ice cream, and mix them into sauces or breadcrumbs for texture. Pepitas are hulled (green) pumpkin seeds; when toasted, they're delicious in salads or as a topping for soup, sweet potatoes, oatmeal, or your favorite grain bowl. Add toasted pine nuts to salads, pilafs, and cooked vegetables, or use them to elevate store-bought hummus. Because pepitas and pine nuts have such a high oil content and therefore go rancid quickly, store them in the freezer. Other nuts can be stored in a cool, dark place.

Whole-milk yogurt

Yogurt is a tangy, creamy vehicle for your morning fruit or granola, but why stop there? You can slather it on flatbread pizzas in place of cheese, or turn it into a dressing or dip flecked with chopped fresh dill or snipped chives. When cooked with cornstarch and egg yolks, it becomes a velvety sauce for meatballs; you can also use it in a marinade or baked goods. In general, regular yogurt is best for sauces and dressings, as it clings well to food. Thicker Greek-style yogurt is ideal for spreads and dips.

PART TWO

GET COOKING

———

37

NEWLYWED
KITCHEN

Ask longtime couples about the best times in their relationships, and many will say the moments they most treasure aren't the obvious ones like their wedding day or other big celebrations. Instead, it's the small details of ordinary days that can mean the most—sharing an after-work cocktail and catching up on the day, or preparing a meal side by side and sitting down at the table to eat.

The recipes gathered here embody that spirit. There are breakfasts for the mornings when you're rushing past each other (fruit smoothies or scones that you've baked ahead and frozen); or for those days when you can linger over another cup of coffee and maybe even have breakfast in bed (glorious egg sandwiches and hearty, good-for-you grain bowls).

The dinner recipes are fast and easy dishes you can put together in no time (as a team or with one of you cooking for the other)—yet they taste like you went to some trouble. Think quick coq au vin or a gently poached salmon with new potatoes and buttermilk dressing; both recipes allow you to walk in the door at six and still eat by seven (and maybe even open a bottle of wine while you're at it).

Within each recipe are the building blocks of good cooking. So as you assemble, say, spicy clams with spaghetti, the two of you will learn how to choose (and clean!) shellfish and how long to boil perfectly al dente pasta. From-scratch pizza will save you from resorting to takeout—again. And because every cook needs a tried-and-true technique to rely on when time is short and people are hungry, there are also several classic main course recipes—chicken paillard, the perfect pan-seared steak, a vegetable frittata, and so on—as well as dozens of flavorful mix-and-match sides. The two parts are meant to complement one another: Choose a main course, then add a side or two. Or make a few sides and call that dinner. There are no rules, only lots of customizable options.

Finally, we collected a dozen or so dessert recipes that you'll want to commit to memory. These are the ones you'll turn to again and again, to serve after dinners for two, to pack for picnics and potlucks, and to proudly present at all manner of momentous occasions. You'll find the classics (chocolate chip cookies, pound cake, fruit crumble) as well as a few that may be new to you (espresso granita, caramel pots de crème, tartufo)—but not for long.

This collection should up the ante when it comes to your cooking skills and provide new go-to recipes for when you're having a busy day, when a big pot of soup and a loaf of crusty bread is all you need, when you want to cook meals ahead that you can freeze and serve later, or when you simply crave mashed potatoes or a fudgy brownie. And, of course, when you want to sit across the table from the person you love and share something delicious.

BREAKFAST

Rise-and-Shine Smoothies

Breakfast Toasts

Maple Granola

Grain Bowls

The Best French Toast

Not-so-Basic
Breakfast Sandwiches

Cream Scones
with Currants

Bacon, Egg, and Toast Cups

Buttermilk Waffles

DINNER

Individual Chicken Potpies

Chicken and Vegetables
in Parchment

Roast Chicken with
Broiled-Vegetable-and-
Bread Salad

Quick Coq au Vin Blanc

Grilled Chicken and
Vegetable Skewers

Mediterranean
Chopped-Chicken Pita

Roasted Quartered
Chicken with Herb Sauce

30-Minute Spaghetti
and Meatballs

Seared Rib-Eye Steak
with Smashed Potatoes

Picadillo-Style Chili

Lamb and Bulgur Stew
with White Beans

Steak and Asparagus
Stir-Fry

Sausage and Mushroom
Burgers with Broccoli Rabe

Spicy-Sausage and Lentil
Stew with Escarole Salad

Spicy Clams with Spaghetti

Poached Salmon with
Potatoes, Cucumber, and
Buttermilk-Dill Dressing

Baked Fish-and-Chips

Paprika Shrimp with
Hummus and Mint

Mussels Steamed with Garlic,
Tomato, and White Wine

Grilled Snapper Sandwiches
with Pickled Vegetables

Fish Stew with Herbed Toasts

Rigatoni with Corn,
Arugula, and Tuna

Farro Risotto with Shrimp

Swordfish with
Watermelon Salad

Tofu with Baby Bok Choy
and Rice Noodles

Orecchiette with Butternut
Squash and Sage

Tortellini Soup with
Peas and Spinach

Ricotta Pizza with Fresh and
Roasted Tomatoes

Minestrone with
Winter Greens

Pasta Caprese

MIX-AND-MATCH MAINS & SIDES

Classic Roast Chicken

Avocado Citrus Salad

Luxurious Mashed Potatoes

Brussels Sprouts Slaw

Minted Couscous

Pan-Fried Steak with Mustard
Cream Sauce

Crushed Peas with Fresh Mint

Honey-Glazed Carrots

Lentil Salad

Roasted Cauliflower with
Shallots and Golden Raisins

Frittata

Creamy Baked Acorn Squash

Chile-Garlic Spinach

Sautéed Mushrooms

Tomato Salad with
Olives and Lemon Zest

Sautéed Sole

Corn and Zucchini
Sauté with Basil

Roasted Asparagus
with Breadcrumbs

Crisp Potatoes
with Rosemary

Cucumber and
Watercress Salad

Pan-Fried Pork Chops

Quinoa-Spinach Pilaf

Chili-Roasted
Sweet Potatoes

Roasted Beets
with Yogurt Sauce

Lemony Braised Broccoli

Chicken Paillards

Iceberg Wedges with
Tahini Dressing

Polenta with Pecorino

Green Beans with
Lime and Mint

Dijon Potato Salad

Caesar Salad

DESSERT

Warm Chocolate
Pudding Cakes

Chocolate Chip Cookies

Rhubarb-Raspberry
Galettes

Classic Shortbread

Lemon Custard Cakes

Blackberry Crumble

Peach Shortcake

Double Chocolate Brownies

Broiled Plums

Perfect Pound Cake

Espresso Granita

Caramel Pots de Crème

Apple Tart

Tartufo for Two

Breakfast

More than two
dozen tasty recipes
and inspired ideas
to jump–start
your day

RISE-AND-SHINE SMOOTHIES

Give your breakfast habit a makeover. Start your day with any of these vibrant, super-healthful smoothies—and put that awesome new blender to good use. As long as you keep a few pantry staples (plain yogurt, fresh or frozen produce, and juice) around the house, you can whip up most of these blended pick-me-ups in seconds. **SERVES 2**

Mango and Yogurt Smoothie

Blend $1/4$ teaspoon ground cinnamon, $1\frac{1}{2}$ cups low-fat plain yogurt, $2\frac{1}{2}$ cups frozen mango chunks, 1 tablespoon honey, and the juice from $1/2$ lime.

Green Machine Smoothie

Blend 6 chopped romaine leaves; 4 kale leaves, ribs removed, chopped; $1/2$ cup flat-leaf parsley sprigs; $1/2$ cup chopped pineapple; $1/2$ cup chopped mango; 1-inch piece fresh ginger, peeled and chopped; and $1\frac{1}{2}$ cups water.

Peanut–Banana–Espresso Smoothie

Blend 1 cup low-fat milk; 1 tablespoon instant espresso powder; $1/4$ cup natural creamy peanut butter; 1 ripe banana, cut into thirds; and 1 cup ice.

Berry–Orange Smoothie

Blend 1 orange, peel and pith removed with a sharp knife, quartered; $1/2$ cup low-fat plain yogurt; $1/2$ cup raspberry sorbet; and $1/2$ cup cranberry juice.

Pineapple and Ginger Smoothie

Blend 1 cup fresh or frozen pineapple, cut into 1-inch pieces; 1-inch piece fresh ginger, peeled and chopped; $1/2$ cup low-fat plain yogurt; 1 cup pineapple juice; $1/8$ teaspoon ground cinnamon; and $1/2$ cup ice (if using fresh pineapple).

Cucumber–Blueberry Smoothie

Blend 1 medium cucumber, peeled, seeded, and cut into 1-inch pieces; 1 cup frozen blueberries; 1 cup white grape juice or pear juice; and $1/2$ cup low-fat plain yogurt.

Pom–Berry Banana Smoothie

Blend 1 orange, peel and pith removed with a sharp knife, quartered; 1 cup frozen mixed berries; 1 ripe banana, cut into thirds; and 1 cup pomegranate juice.

BREAKFAST TOASTS

Not that there's anything wrong with good old buttered toast, but we'd much rather see these inspired combos on our breakfast table. Try an irresistible version of the now–ubiquitous avocado toast, or cover slices of crusty bread with combinations like ricotta, dates, and honey; smoked trout, butter, and red onion; or labneh, roasted plums, and almonds. The possibilities are endless, and so are the thanks you'll get from your spouse. Keep these ideas in mind for future brunch guests as well. **SERVES 2**

1. Top toasted bread with chopped or mashed avocado, toasted coriander seeds, fresh cilantro leaves, and lemon zest.

2. Butter toasted bread. Top with flaked smoked trout, capers, and thinly sliced red onion.

3. Layer thin slices of ham, fontina cheese, and pear on toasted bread; sprinkle with freshly ground pepper.

4. Top toasted bread with cooked bacon and sliced grape tomatoes; sprinkle with chopped fresh flat-leaf parsley.

5. Spread soft goat cheese on toasted bread. Top with sliced radish and sprouts; season with coarse salt and freshly ground pepper.

6. Spread nut butter on toasted bread. Top with sliced banana and toasted coconut flakes.

7. Spread ricotta cheese on grain bread. Top with slivered dates and drizzle with honey.

8. Spread mustard on toasted bread. Top with sliced salami and cucumbers, and chopped fresh dill.

9. Spread hummus on toasted bread. Top with thinly sliced cheddar and sprigs of mint.

10. Spread labneh on toasted bread. Top with roasted plums and chopped almonds.

MAPLE GRANOLA

Granola comes in endless variations, but this irresistible take on the classic
is destined to become your household go–to. Packed with a toasty mix of rolled
oats, nuts, and dried coconut, and sweetened with pure maple syrup, it gets
an addictively savory edge from a teaspoon of salt. **MAKES 7 CUPS**

3 cups old-fashioned rolled oats	½ cup packed light-brown sugar
1 cup dried unsweetened coconut chips	¼ cup sesame seeds
1 cup pecans or walnuts, coarsely chopped	1 teaspoon coarse salt
½ cup pure maple syrup	¾ teaspoon freshly grated nutmeg
½ cup extra-virgin olive oil	½ cup golden raisins

Preheat oven to 300°F. In a large bowl, mix together oats, coconut, nuts, syrup, oil, brown sugar,
sesame seeds, salt, and nutmeg. Spread granola in an even layer on a rimmed baking sheet.
Bake 40 minutes, stirring every 10 minutes. Add raisins and bake until granola is toasted, about
10 minutes more. Let cool completely. (Store granola in an airtight container for up to 2 weeks.)

GRAIN BOWLS

These hearty breakfast bowls are a dream to wake up to and a giant step up from instant oatmeal. Start with any cooked whole grain, then top it with a combination of natural ingredients. Experimenting with different combinations is (at least) half the fun. You can go sweet or savory, and swap any whole grain (brown rice, farro, freekah, barley—you name it) for the suggestions here. **SERVES 2**

Black Rice with Smoked Salmon, Red Onion, and Dill

1. In a heavy-bottomed pot, bring ½ cup black rice and ¾ cup water to a boil. Cover, reduce heat, and simmer until rice is tender and water has been absorbed, about 45 minutes. Remove from heat; let stand 10 minutes. Let cool slightly.
2. Divide cooked rice between two bowls. Top with 2 ounces smoked salmon and thinly sliced red onion, dividing evenly. Sprinkle with sesame seeds, top with fresh dill, and serve.

Quinoa with Bacons and Eggs

1. In a saucepan, toast ½ cup quinoa over medium-high heat until golden, 1 to 2 minutes. Add ¾ cup water and ¼ teaspoon salt, and stir; bring to a boil. Cover, reduce heat, and cook until quinoa is tender but still chewy and has absorbed all the liquid, about 15 minutes. Fluff quinoa with a fork.
2. Meanwhile, in a heavy-bottomed skillet, cook 4 slices bacon over medium heat until crisp, about 4 minutes, flipping once. Drain on a paper towel–lined plate, then chop. Fry 2 large eggs in same skillet, until whites are set around yolks and golden around the edges, about 3 minutes.
3. Divide quinoa between two bowls. Top each with an egg, sprinkle with chopped bacon, and season with hot sauce.

Kasha with Banana, Coconut, and Pecans

1. Preheat oven to 350°F. Place ¼ cup coconut flakes and ¼ cup pecans in a single layer on a rimmed baking sheet and toast until fragrant and just golden, about 5 minutes.
2. Meanwhile, bring 1 cup water and ¼ teaspoon coarse salt to a boil in a saucepan. Whisk in ½ cup kasha. Return to a boil. Cover, reduce heat, and simmer until tender, 5 to 7 minutes.
3. Divide kasha between two bowls. Slice ½ banana over each bowl, garnish with toasted coconut flakes and pecans, dividing evenly, and drizzle with maple syrup to taste.

THE BEST FRENCH TOAST

Everyone loves French toast. This one is easy enough for weekdays but special enough for Sunday brunch. Top with fresh fruit, or, if you're feeling particularly indulgent, add a few strips of bacon alongside (with extra maple syrup for dipping, of course). **SERVES 2**

3	large eggs
¾	cup milk
	Juice of ½ medium orange (about 2 tablespoons)
1	tablespoon pure vanilla extract
1½	teaspoons granulated sugar
¼	teaspoon ground cinnamon
	Pinch of freshly grated nutmeg

	Pinch of salt
4	slices bread, 1 inch thick, preferably day-old
2	tablespoons unsalted butter, plus more for serving
2	tablespoons vegetable oil
	Confectioners' sugar, for serving
	Pure maple syrup, for serving

1. Whisk together eggs, milk, juice, vanilla, granulated sugar, cinnamon, nutmeg, and salt in a bowl.

2. Place bread in a shallow baking pan large enough to hold bread slices in a single layer. Pour egg mixture over bread and soak 10 minutes. Turn slices over and soak 10 minutes more, or until soaked through.

3. Preheat oven to 200°F. Place a wire rack on a rimmed baking sheet. Heat butter and oil in a large skillet over medium. Fry bread slices until golden brown, 2 to 3 minutes per side. Transfer to wire rack and keep in oven until ready to serve. Top with confectioners' sugar and a pat of butter, and serve warm with maple syrup.

NOT-SO-BASIC BREAKFAST SANDWICHES

There are few, if any, more satisfying
breakfasts than the egg-and-cheese-
on-a-roll (in all of its many forms).
If you're looking to stretch your
repertoire, start with any one of these
five delicious ideas. Learn to make
them all, then start adding your own
spins. You're sure to have breakfast
firmly in hand. **SERVES 2**

**See pages 52—53
for recipes.**

NOT-SO-BASIC BREAKFAST SANDWICHES

Prosciutto, Tomato, Basil, and Scrambled Eggs on Toast

2   large eggs

2   tablespoons heavy cream or milk

    Coarse salt and freshly ground pepper

1   teaspoon unsalted butter, plus more for toast

2   slices sourdough bread, toasted

1   tomato, cut crosswise into 1/2-inch-thick slices

6   slices prosciutto (about 1/8 pound)

    Fresh basil leaves, for serving

1. With a fork, beat together eggs and cream in a bowl; season with salt and pepper.

2. Melt butter in a nonstick skillet over medium heat. Add egg mixture; using a heatproof flexible spatula, gently pull eggs to center of pan and let liquid parts run out under the perimeter. Cook until eggs are just set, 1 1/2 to 2 minutes.

3. Butter each toasted bread slice, and top with sliced tomato, prosciutto, eggs, and basil leaves. Season with salt and pepper, and serve immediately.

Photographs on pages 50–51.

Fried Green Tomato and Egg on Buttermilk Biscuit

1   large, firm green tomato, cut crosswise into 1/2-inch thick slices

    Coarse salt and freshly ground pepper

1/4   cup yellow cornmeal, preferably stone-ground

3   large eggs

1/4   cup vegetable oil, for frying

1   tablespoon unsalted butter

2   buttermilk biscuits (see recipe for Peach Shortcake, page 158; omit sugar)

1. Season tomato slices with salt and pepper. Place cornmeal in a bowl. Lightly beat 1 egg in another bowl.

2. Heat oil in a skillet over medium. Dip tomato slices in beaten egg and dredge in cornmeal. Working in batches, fry tomatoes in a single layer until golden brown, about 3 minutes per side. Transfer to paper towels to drain.

3. Melt butter in another skillet over medium heat. When butter begins to sizzle, crack 1 egg into pan. Cook until white is beginning to set, then use the edge of a spatula to break yolk. Continue cooking until white is light golden underneath, 2 to 3 minutes, spooning butter over yolk to cook it. Season with salt and pepper. Repeat with remaining egg.

4. Split biscuits, and sandwich each with an egg and a few fried tomato rounds. Serve immediately.

Boiled Egg, Harissa, and Yogurt on Pita

1   (6- or 8-inch) pita bread, split in half crosswise

       Extra-virgin olive oil, for brushing

½   teaspoon za'atar spice blend

2   large eggs

2   tablespoons plain yogurt or labneh

1   tablespoon harissa paste

       Fresh cilantro, for serving

1. Preheat oven to 400°F. Brush split sides of pita generously with oil and sprinkle evenly with za'atar. Bake until crisp and just golden, about 10 minutes.

2. Meanwhile, place eggs in a deep saucepan and cover with cold water by 1 inch. Bring to a boil over high heat, then immediately remove from heat, cover, and let stand 12 minutes. Use a slotted spoon to transfer eggs to an ice-water bath in order to stop the cooking. Let cool; then peel and slice.

3. Top each pita round with 1 tablespoon yogurt, 1 egg, half the harissa, and cilantro. Serve immediately.

Egg in a Bagel Hole

1   tablespoon unsalted butter

1   bagel, sliced in half crosswise

2   large eggs

       Coarse salt and freshly ground black pepper

       Red-pepper flakes, for serving

       Fresh flat-leaf parsley, for serving

1. Melt butter in a large nonstick or cast-iron skillet over medium heat. Toast bagel halves, cut-side down, in skillet until lightly golden. Crack each egg into a small bowl or spouted cup, and pour into a bagel hole. Season with salt and black pepper.

2. Cover skillet and continue cooking eggs until set, about 3 minutes (or longer or shorter, depending on how runny—or not—you like your eggs). Transfer each bagel half to a plate, and top eggs with salt, red-pepper flakes, and parsley.

Spinach and Soft–Boiled Egg on Toast

1½   teaspoons olive oil

1   garlic clove, thinly sliced

1   bunch flat-leaf spinach, trimmed and washed, with some water still clinging

       Coarse salt and freshly ground pepper

2   large eggs

2   slices rustic bread, toasted and buttered

1. Heat oil in a skillet over medium. Add garlic; cook, stirring, until fragrant and beginning to brown, about 1 minute. Add spinach gradually, waiting for one batch to wilt before adding the next. Cook, tossing, until tender, 3 to 4 minutes. Season with salt and pepper.

2. Meanwhile, place eggs in a deep saucepan and cover with cold water by 1 inch. Bring to a boil over high heat, then immediately remove from heat, cover, and let stand 4 to 6 minutes. Use a slotted spoon to transfer eggs to an ice-water bath in order to stop the cooking.

3. Top each piece of buttered toast with spinach, dividing evenly. Hold an egg over toast, tap around center with a knife, and gently pull shell apart; with a spoon, scoop out egg on top of spinach. Season with salt and pepper.

CREAM SCONES WITH CURRANTS

Scones take mere minutes to prepare, and the basic formula lends itself to variations of all kinds—sweet and savory. The key is to use a light hand when mixing the dough and cutting it into squares, so the butter stays in pieces and produces the flakiest pastries. Scones also freeze really well, making this recipe a perfect candidate for Sunday baking. Just reheat them straight from the freezer in a low oven for about 15 minutes, and you're good to go. **MAKES 6**

VARIATIONS

Chocolate-Chunk Coconut
Omit currants; replace with ¾ cup coconut flakes and ½ cup chopped chocolate.

Lemon-Ginger
Omit currants; replace with ⅓ cup diced candied ginger and 1 teaspoon grated lemon zest.

Cherry-Hazelnut
Add ½ teaspoon cinnamon to flour mixture. Omit currants; replace with 1 cup chopped skinned hazelnuts and ⅔ cup dried cherries.

Cheddar-Chive
Omit sugar and currants; replace with ¾ cup grated sharp cheddar and 2 tablespoons snipped chives.

¾ cup plus 1 tablespoon cold heavy cream	½ teaspoon salt
1 large egg	6 tablespoons cold unsalted butter, cut into small pieces
2 cups all-purpose flour, plus more for surface	⅔ cup dried currants
¼ cup granulated sugar	Sanding sugar (optional)
2 teaspoons baking powder	

1. Preheat oven to 400°F. In a small bowl, whisk together ¾ cup cream and the egg. In a large bowl, whisk together flour, granulated sugar, baking powder, and salt.

2. With a pastry blender or two knives, cut butter into flour mixture until it resembles coarse meal, with a few pea-size pieces of butter remaining. Stir in currants. With a fork, stir in cream mixture until just combined. (The dough should be crumbly; do not overwork.)

3. Transfer dough to a lightly floured work surface and pat into a 4-by-6-inch rectangle. With a bench scraper or a sharp knife, cut into 6 (2-inch) squares and transfer to a parchment-lined baking sheet. Brush tops with remaining tablespoon cream and sprinkle with sanding sugar, if desired. Bake until golden, rotating sheet halfway through, 16 to 18 minutes.

BACON, EGG, AND TOAST CUPS

Upgrade the classic American breakfast from basic to impressive with this fun serving idea. We used bacon, but you can substitute sausage or make a vegetarian version with sautéed spinach. **MAKES 4**

2   tablespoons unsalted butter, melted

4   slices white or whole-wheat sandwich bread

4   slices bacon

4   large eggs

Coarse salt and freshly ground pepper

1. Preheat oven to 375°F. Lightly butter 4 standard muffin cups. With a rolling pin, flatten bread slices slightly and, with a 4¼-inch cookie cutter, cut 4 rounds. Cut each round in half, then press 2 halves into each muffin cup, overlapping slightly and making sure bread comes up to edge of cup. Use extra bread to patch any gaps. Brush bread with remaining butter.

2. In a large skillet, cook bacon over medium heat until almost crisp, about 4 minutes, flipping once. (It will continue to cook in the oven.) Lay 1 bacon slice in each bread cup and crack an egg over each. Season with salt and pepper. Bake until egg whites are just set, 20 to 25 minutes. Run a small knife around cups to loosen toasts. Serve immediately.

BUTTERMILK WAFFLES

On weekday mornings when you're both trying to get out the door, making waffles from scratch might seem like way too much work. But prepare these in advance and freeze them, and you can have a weekend–worthy breakfast any day of the week. Just be sure to keep an eye on the waffle iron: If the waffles start turning dark brown, lower the heat; if they're looking too pale, turn it up or increase the cooking time. **SERVES 4**

2	cups all-purpose flour	2	cups low-fat buttermilk
2	tablespoons sugar	½	cup (1 stick) unsalted butter, melted
2	teaspoons baking powder	2	large eggs
1	teaspoon baking soda		Vegetable oil, for waffle iron
½	teaspoon salt		Butter and pure maple syrup, for serving

1. Preheat oven to 275°F; set a rack on a rimmed baking sheet and place in oven. In a medium bowl, whisk together flour, sugar, baking powder, baking soda, and salt. In a large bowl, whisk together buttermilk, butter, and eggs; add flour mixture and mix just until batter is combined.

2. Heat waffle iron according to manufacturer's instructions; brush with oil. Pour about ½ cup batter onto iron (or adjust amount according to iron's size), and cook until waffles are golden brown and crisp, 3 to 5 minutes. Transfer to rack in oven to keep warm; repeat with remaining batter. Serve waffles with butter and maple syrup.

Dinner

Quick, easy, and flavorful meals to cook and enjoy together

INDIVIDUAL CHICKEN POTPIES

These buttery, golden-crusted chicken potpies have undeniable eye appeal, and they make a delectable comfort-food dinner for winter nights. You will have leftover puff pastry, which you can freeze and use later to make appetizers and fruit tarts. Or, feel free to double this recipe to make and freeze more potpies. **SERVES 2**

1	package (17.3 ounces) frozen puff pastry, preferably all butter, thawed
2	tablespoons all-purpose flour, plus more for surface
2	tablespoons unsalted butter
½	onion, diced
1	small carrot, thinly sliced
1	stalk celery, thinly sliced
1	small Yukon Gold potato, scrubbed and cut into ½-inch dice

1¼	cups low-sodium chicken broth
1	cup collard-green leaves, tough stems and ribs removed, coarsely chopped
8	ounces boneless, skinless chicken breast, cut into 1-inch chunks
	Coarse salt and freshly ground pepper
1	large egg, lightly beaten

1. Preheat oven to 425°F. Roll out 1 sheet puff pastry on a lightly floured surface. Cut 2 rounds to fit ramekins, ½ inch larger all around than dishes. Cut a small X in center of each to allow steam to vent. Refrigerate rounds on a parchment-lined baking sheet.

2. Melt butter in a large skillet over medium heat. Add onion. Cook, stirring, until soft, about 4 minutes. Add carrot, celery, and potato. Cook, stirring, until soft, about 6 minutes. Stir in flour, then broth; bring to a boil. Add greens and chicken. Simmer until sauce is thickened, about 2 minutes; season with salt and pepper.

3. Divide mixture evenly between dishes. Top with pastry, press edges to seal, and brush with egg. Bake on a baking sheet until golden, about 25 minutes.

CHICKEN AND VEGETABLES IN PARCHMENT

Dinner at home feels like an extra-special occasion when you serve up parcels of parchment-wrapped chicken with vegetables and herbs. This recipe is a nice introduction to a cooking technique that won't be intimidating at all once you try it—and soon enough, you'll start using the parchment technique for fish, too. It's a win-win: The method intensifies flavors with very little added fat. **SERVES 2**

½ pound baby bok choy, trimmed, leaves separated

6 ounces cherry tomatoes, halved

1 small shallot, thinly sliced

½ bunch fresh thyme

1 tablespoon extra-virgin olive oil

Coarse salt and freshly ground pepper

2 boneless, skinless chicken-breast halves (about 6 ounces each), pounded ½ inch thick (see page 141)

2 tablespoons dry white wine, such as Sauvignon Blanc

1. Preheat oven to 400°F with racks in upper and lower thirds. Cut two 12-by-17-inch pieces of parchment. Fold each in half crosswise to make a crease, then unfold and lay them flat. Toss together bok choy leaves, tomatoes, shallot, ½ teaspoon thyme leaves, and oil in a large bowl. Season with salt and pepper.

2. Season chicken with salt and pepper. Divide bok choy mixture evenly and place half on one side of crease on each piece of parchment, then top with chicken and 2 thyme sprigs. Drizzle each with 1 tablespoon wine. Fold parchment over, then make small overlapping pleats to seal and create half-moon-shaped packets.

3. Bake on a rimmed baking sheet until packets are puffed, about 22 minutes (chicken should be cooked through). Transfer to plates; serve immediately, carefully cutting packets open with kitchen shears so as to avoid getting burned by steam.

ROAST CHICKEN WITH BROILED-VEGETABLE-AND-BREAD SALAD

This is our take on the legendary roast chicken with bread salad at San Francisco's Zuni Café. The recipe makes enough for a second meal, so the two of you can enjoy it the next day—or keep it in mind for company. **SERVES 4**

1 whole chicken (3¼ to 3½ pounds)	4 slices (2 inches thick) rustic Italian bread
Coarse salt and freshly ground pepper	1 garlic clove, halved
6 thyme sprigs	2 small eggplants or 4 Japanese eggplants (1½ pounds), cut into 1½-inch wedges
Extra-virgin olive oil	2 red bell peppers, quartered lengthwise and seeded
2 tablespoons fresh lemon juice	
1 tablespoon red-wine vinegar	3 large Swiss chard leaves, tough stems and ribs removed, leaves torn into bite-size pieces (3 cups)
1 tablespoon capers, rinsed	

1. Sprinkle chicken with 1 tablespoon salt and season with pepper. Gently slip your fingers under skin. Stuff thyme under skin of breast and thighs and in cavity. Let chicken stand at least 1 hour before roasting.

2. Preheat oven to 475°F. Place a baking pan or ovenproof skillet just large enough to fit chicken in oven for 5 minutes. Pat chicken dry, then place, breast side up, in hot baking pan. Roast, rotating pan and basting with drippings once, until skin is golden and chicken registers 160°F in the thickest part of thigh, 40 to 45 minutes. Let rest at least 15 minutes, then carve. Skim fat from juices in baking pan. Pour remaining juices (about 2 tablespoons) into a measuring cup; add oil to come to ¼ cup. Whisk in lemon juice and vinegar. Add capers and 1 teaspoon salt; season with pepper.

3. Heat broiler with rack 8 inches from the heat source. Drizzle bread slices with oil. Toast until browned on both sides. While warm, rub with cut sides of garlic. Tear into bite-size pieces; place in a large bowl. Drizzle eggplant and peppers with oil, season with salt and pepper, and toss to coat. Spread onto 2 rimmed baking sheets; broil until browned and tender, 10 to 12 minutes, flipping vegetables halfway through. Cut into bite-size pieces; add to bowl. Add chard, toss all together, pour on three-quarters of the dressing, and toss again. Transfer to a platter and top with chicken. Serve remaining dressing on the side.

QUICK COQ AU VIN BLANC

Our one-hour coq au vin will save you loads of time in the kitchen, without sacrificing any of the flavor of the French classic. (The usual method involves cutting up a whole chicken, and can take up to four hours to cook.) This version uses just the chicken thighs, and white wine instead of red makes it "blanc." Bonus: If you haven't done much braising yet, consider this your introduction to the foolproof technique. **SERVES 2**

2 slices bacon, cut into ½-inch pieces	1 tablespoon tomato paste
4 bone-in, skin-on chicken thighs	1 cup dry white wine
Coarse salt and freshly ground pepper	1 cup low-sodium chicken broth
2 tablespoons all-purpose flour, for sprinkling	Cooked egg noodles tossed with olive oil or butter, for serving
5 ounces frozen pearl onions, thawed and drained	¼ cup lightly packed fresh flat-leaf parsley leaves, chopped, for serving
4 ounces cremini mushrooms, halved (quartered, if large)	

1. Preheat oven to 350°F. Brown bacon in a large, straight-sided ovenproof skillet over medium-high heat until fat is rendered, about 5 minutes. With a slotted spoon, transfer to a plate. Season chicken with salt and pepper; sprinkle with flour. Add to skillet, skin-side down; cook until golden, about 4 minutes per side. Transfer to plate. Remove all but 1 tablespoon fat from skillet.

2. Reduce heat to medium. Add onions and mushrooms; season with salt. Cook until golden in spots, about 10 minutes. Stir in tomato paste; cook 30 seconds. Add wine; boil until evaporated, about 8 minutes. Add broth and bring to a boil. Return chicken and juices to skillet; top with bacon. Cook uncovered in oven until a thermometer inserted into thickest part of chicken (without touching bone) registers 165°F, about 20 minutes. Serve over noodles and sprinkle with parsley.

GRILLED CHICKEN AND VEGETABLE SKEWERS

These year–round favorites couldn't be simpler to make: The only seasonings you need are salt, pepper, olive oil, lemon, and parsley. Throw the skewers on the grill in the summer or broil them anytime. You can swap in any skewer–worthy vegetables you like, such as bell peppers, but be sure to keep all the pieces the same size so they'll cook evenly. Soon you'll be using your metal skewers to whip up party snacks, fast weeknight dinners, and weekend lunches. **SERVES 2**

¾ to 1	pound boneless, skinless chicken thighs, cut into 1½-inch-wide strips
2	tablespoons extra-virgin olive oil, plus more for dressing
	Coarse salt and freshly ground pepper
1	medium zucchini, cut crosswise into 1-inch-thick rounds
8	medium cipollini onions
8	medium cremini mushrooms, trimmed
	Grated zest and juice of ½ lemon
¼	cup coarsely chopped fresh flat-leaf parsley leaves

1. Heat grill (or grill pan) over medium-high (if using a charcoal grill, coals are ready when you can hold your hand 5 inches above grill for just 3 to 4 seconds). Meanwhile, in a bowl, toss chicken with 1 tablespoon oil; season with salt and pepper. In a separate bowl, toss vegetables with remaining tablespoon oil; season with salt and pepper. Divide chicken evenly among 2 metal skewers. Arrange each vegetable separately on skewers.

2. Place onion skewers on grill and cook 5 minutes. Add chicken and zucchini skewers; cook, turning occasionally, 5 minutes. Add mushroom skewers; cook until chicken and vegetables are cooked through and charred in places, about 10 minutes.

3. Dress with lemon zest and juice, oil, and parsley. (Skewers can be assembled and refrigerated up to 3 hours ahead; let sit at room temperature 30 minutes before grilling.)

MEDITERRANEAN CHOPPED-CHICKEN PITA

Somewhere between an open-face sandwich and a pizza, this chopped-chicken pita gets much of its deliciously smoky flavor from the grill. Both the chicken and the pita go right onto the grill until they're slightly charred, and then you simply layer the bread with the hummus, chicken, fresh vegetables, and cheese. Serve this for lunch, dinner, or as a snack—and watch it vanish instantly. **SERVES 2**

½   pound boneless, skinless chicken-breast halves (about 2 halves)

Extra-virgin olive oil, for brushing and drizzling

Coarse salt and freshly ground pepper

2   (6-inch) pitas

⅔   cup plain store-bought hummus

½   cup cherry tomatoes, halved

1   scallion, trimmed and thinly sliced

¼   small head radicchio, thinly sliced

¼   cup crumbled feta (about 1 ounce)

Microgreens, for serving

1. Heat grill (or grill pan) to medium-high (if using a charcoal grill, coals are ready when you can hold your hand 5 inches above grill for just 3 to 4 seconds). Brush chicken with oil; season with salt and pepper. Brush grates with oil. Grill chicken, turning once, until cooked through and lightly marked in spots, 6 to 8 minutes total. Transfer to a cutting board. When cool enough to handle, cut into bite-size pieces.

2. Brush both sides of each pita with oil. Grill, flipping once, until lightly marked and crisp, 4 to 5 minutes. Spread hummus on one side of each pita. Top with chicken, tomatoes, scallion, radicchio, feta, and microgreens. Drizzle with oil and serve.

ROASTED QUARTERED CHICKEN WITH HERB SAUCE

It's not only a mainstay for Sunday supper: A quartered chicken roasts in just half an hour on any old weeknight. Since the bird is cut up, it has more exposed skin than a whole chicken, leading to more irresistible crispiness all over. When the bird is hot out of the oven, its toasty skin melds with the savory herb sauce for the most intense flavor. Serve the chicken alongside diced potatoes roasted to crunchy French fry—like perfection (see recipe on page 135). **SERVES 4**

1   whole chicken (about 4 pounds), quartered and backbone removed (see tip below), room temperature

¼   cup plus 1 tablespoon extra-virgin olive oil

    Coarse salt and freshly ground black pepper

2   tablespoons red-wine vinegar

1   cup packed fresh flat-leaf parsley leaves, chopped

½   teaspoon minced garlic

½   teaspoon red-pepper flakes

1. Preheat oven to 450°F. Pat chicken dry with paper towels. Rub chicken with 1 tablespoon oil; season with salt and black pepper. Arrange, skin-side up, on a rimmed baking sheet. Roast until golden and a thermometer inserted into thickest part of breast (without touching bone) registers 160°F, about 30 minutes.

2. Transfer chicken to a plate. Pour off and discard fat from baking sheet; return chicken to sheet. Whisk together remaining ¼ cup oil, the vinegar, parsley, garlic, and red-pepper flakes in a bowl. Season with salt. Spoon sauce over chicken, and let stand 10 minutes before serving with accumulated pan juices and sauce.

TIP

To quarter a chicken: Turn it breast–side up. Gently pull leg away from body, then slice between thigh and body to reveal hip socket; cut through joint to remove leg. Repeat with remaining leg. To remove backbone: Lift up chicken and cut downward through rib cage and then shoulder joints to separate breast from back (save backbone for making stock). Split the breast by slicing along either side of bone in center, cutting through rib cage. Halve wishbone with heel of knife. Separate breast halves.

30-MINUTE SPAGHETTI AND MEATBALLS

You might think a proper meatball needs to simmer all afternoon, ideally on a nonna's stovetop. But meatballs actually don't need that much time—or very many ingredients—to cook. You can make delicious ones in less than half an hour: Just cook them through in a simple tomato sauce (the only herb you need is fresh parsley). Be sure to put the pasta water on to boil while you cook the meatballs so they're ready at the same time, then serve with a bottle of Barbera or Montepulciano. This recipe makes enough meatballs for more than one meal; serve leftovers in sandwiches. **SERVES 2, WITH LEFTOVERS**

Coarse salt and freshly ground pepper

¼ cup finely grated Parmigiano-Reggiano (1 ounce), plus more for serving

¼ cup chopped fresh flat-leaf parsley

2 garlic cloves, minced

1 large egg

1 pound ground beef chuck (80% lean)

¼ cup plain dried breadcrumbs

1 tablespoon olive oil

1 can (28 ounces) crushed tomatoes in puree

8 ounces spaghetti

1. Bring a large pot of salted water to boil. In a bowl, combine Parmesan, parsley, garlic, egg, 1 teaspoon salt, and 1 teaspoon pepper. Add beef and breadcrumbs; mix gently. Form into 16 balls.

2. In a 5-quart Dutch oven or heavy pot, heat oil over medium. Add meatballs and cook, turning until browned, 8 to 10 minutes. Add tomatoes; bring to a boil. Reduce to a simmer; cover partially and cook, stirring occasionally, until meatballs are cooked through, 10 to 12 minutes.

3. Meanwhile, cook pasta until al dente according to package instructions. Drain and return to pot; add meatballs and sauce, and toss gently. Serve with Parmesan.

SEARED RIB-EYE STEAK WITH SMASHED POTATOES

There's really not much to this recipe. You sear the rib-eye on the stovetop first to give it a great crust, then finish it in the oven so the steak cooks through evenly without burning the exterior. Serve the rib-eye with a side of thyme-flavored smashed potatoes: They're fun to make (you literally smash the potatoes with your hands), and they round out the dinner perfectly. **SERVES 2**

---

1   pound small potatoes, preferably in a mix of colors, scrubbed

    Coarse salt and freshly ground pepper

2   tablespoons plus 1 teaspoon extra-virgin olive oil

4   sprigs thyme

1   tablespoon unsalted butter, room temperature

½   scallion, trimmed and thinly sliced

1   (2-pound) bone-in rib-eye steak (about 2 inches thick), room temperature

1. Preheat oven to 425°F. In a large pot, bring potatoes to a boil in generously salted water. Reduce heat to a simmer and cook until fork-tender, about 8 minutes. Drain and let cool slightly. Brush a rimmed baking sheet with 1 tablespoon oil. Lightly crush each potato on sheet with palm to ½-inch thickness. Brush with 1 tablespoon oil. Season with salt and pepper, and scatter thyme on top. Roast, rotating sheet halfway through, until golden and crisp, about 25 minutes. Keep the oven on.

2. Combine butter and scallion in a bowl. Season with salt. Heat a large cast-iron or other heavy skillet over medium-high for 2 minutes. Pat steak dry and rub with remaining teaspoon oil. Season generously with salt and pepper, and place in hot pan. Cook until browned, about 5 minutes a side. Transfer skillet to oven. Roast alongside potatoes until a thermometer inserted in thickest part of steak reads 130°F for medium-rare, 10 to 12 minutes. Transfer steak to a platter, top with scallion butter, and let rest 10 minutes before slicing. Serve sliced steak with smashed potatoes.

PICADILLO-STYLE CHILI

Break out of your ground-beef routine with this wonderfully spicy, garlicky, unexpected chili recipe. Inspired by classic Cuban *picadillo* sauce, it brings together ingredients you might not normally put in chili—cumin, red-wine vinegar, almonds, olives, currants—but can easily find in your pantry or grocery store. The dish is customizable, too: Adjust the toppings to your—or your partner's— liking. **SERVES 2**

1 tablespoon extra-virgin olive oil	1 pound ground beef (80% lean)
¼ cup chopped garlic (from 6 cloves)	Coarse salt
½ large onion, chopped (¾ cup)	1½ tablespoons red-wine vinegar
1 poblano chile, chopped, ribs and seeds removed if less heat is desired	1 can (14.5 ounces) whole peeled tomatoes in juice, chopped
1 teaspoon ground cumin	Cooked rice, sliced green olives (such as manzanilla), chopped toasted almonds, and currants, for serving
¼ teaspoon ground cinnamon	

1. Heat oil in a large pot over medium-high. Add garlic, onion, and chile; cook, stirring occasionally, until softened, about 5 minutes. Add cumin and cinnamon; cook, stirring constantly, just until fragrant, about 1 minute.

2. Add beef and season with salt. Cook, breaking up meat, until browned, about 5 minutes. Add vinegar and tomatoes with their juices; season with salt. Bring to a boil, then reduce heat and simmer, stirring occasionally, until thickened, about 10 minutes. Serve over rice with olives, almonds, and currants.

LAMB AND BULGUR STEW WITH WHITE BEANS

A small amount of lamb (just a half pound) goes a long way in this stew, which uses meat more as a condiment than a main ingredient. Much of the flavor and heft comes from healthful, affordable ingredients like bulgur, white beans, spinach, and feta. The recipe is fairly quick and fuss-free, too: It only takes about 40 minutes from start to finish. Leftovers are fantastic reheated the next day (and even the day after that!). **SERVES 2, WITH LEFTOVERS**

2	tablespoons extra-virgin olive oil
1	onion, finely chopped
½	pound ground lamb
⅔	cup bulgur
¾	teaspoon red-pepper flakes
	Coarse salt and freshly ground black pepper
2	teaspoons sweet paprika

1	can (28 ounces) diced plum tomatoes
2	cups water
1	can (14.5 ounces) gigante or cannellini beans, rinsed and drained
5	ounces baby spinach (about 5 cups)
3½	ounces feta cheese (about ⅔ cup), plus more for garnish
1	tablespoon fresh oregano leaves, plus more for garnish

1. Heat oil in a large pot over medium-high. Add onion, lamb, bulgur, red-pepper flakes, 1½ teaspoons salt, and ½ teaspoon black pepper. Cook, stirring to break up lamb, until lamb is cooked, about 5 minutes. Add paprika; stir until fragrant and toasted, about 30 seconds. Add tomatoes and water, bring to a simmer, and cover. Lower heat; cook, stirring occasionally, until bulgur is tender, about 25 minutes.

2. Stir in beans, spinach, feta, and oregano; cook until feta is almost melted and beans are warmed through, about 2 minutes. Garnish with more feta and oregano.

STEAK AND ASPARAGUS STIR-FRY

When you're pressed for time or just in the mood for a no-fuss dinner, a stir-fry is the way to go. This one stars spicy chiles, fresh asparagus, and either skirt steak or New York strip. Skirt steak is an ideal cut for stir-frying because it's long and thin (read: easy to slice) with a loose-grained texture that soaks up the pan juices; New York strip steak is a pricier alternative with similar qualities. Whichever cut you use, make sure to slice it against the grain—breaking up those visible, overly chewy muscle fibers that run from one end of the steak to the other. Leftovers reheat beautifully. **SERVES 2, GENEROUSLY**

2	tablespoons safflower oil
9	ounces skirt steak, cut with the grain into 4-inch-long pieces, then against the grain into ¼-inch-thick slices; or New York strip steak, cut against the grain into ¼-inch-thick slices
	Coarse salt
1	(1½-inch) piece of peeled fresh ginger, minced (about 3 tablespoons)
1½	red Thai chiles or ½ jalapeño chile, minced, seeds and ribs included
1½	bunches scallions, trimmed and thinly sliced on the diagonal, white and green parts separated
1½	bunches asparagus (about 1½ pounds), trimmed and sliced on the diagonal into 2 inch-long pieces
	Cooked rice, lime wedges, and dry-roasted peanuts, for serving

1. Heat a large wok or skillet over high. Add 1 tablespoon oil, swirl to coat, and add steak. Season with salt and sear, stirring occasionally, until golden brown, about 3 minutes. Transfer to a plate.

2. Add remaining tablespoon oil to wok and swirl to coat. Add ginger, chiles, and scallion whites, and cook, stirring, 30 seconds. Add asparagus and cook until crisp-tender, about 2 minutes. Return steak to wok along with scallion greens. Toss to combine and heat through. Remove from heat and season with salt. Serve over rice, with lime wedges and peanuts.

SAUSAGE AND MUSHROOM BURGERS WITH BROCCOLI RABE

You can call these sausage burgers, or think of them as a spin on Philadelphia–style roast pork and broccoli rabe sandwiches. Either way, they pack more flavor than your average burger (or sandwich), and they're destined to become household favorites. The recipe makes four, but if it'll be just the two of you for lunch or dinner, you can easily halve the ingredients. The burgers taste best straight out of the pan, so don't bother making extra—unless you have room for seconds. **MAKES 4**

3 tablespoons extra-virgin olive oil	¼ teaspoon red-pepper flakes, plus more for sprinkling
12 ounces cremini mushrooms, finely chopped	1 pound sweet Italian sausage, removed from casing
Coarse salt and freshly ground black pepper	4 slices provolone
12 ounces (1 bunch) broccoli rabe, cut into 2-inch pieces	4 Portuguese or ciabatta rolls, halved crosswise and lightly toasted
2 tablespoons fresh lemon juice	Mayonnaise, for serving

1. Heat 1 tablespoon oil in a large nonstick skillet over medium-high. Add mushrooms; season with salt. Cook, stirring occasionally, until golden brown, about 5 minutes. Transfer to a bowl. Heat 1 more tablespoon oil in skillet over medium-high. Add broccoli rabe; season with salt. Cook until crisp-tender, about 4 minutes. Stir in lemon juice and red-pepper flakes. Transfer to another bowl.

2. Wipe skillet clean. Stir together sausage and mushrooms; season with salt and pepper. Form into 4 patties. Heat remaining tablespoon oil in skillet over medium-high. Cook patties, flipping once, until just cooked through, about 6 minutes. Top each with cheese, cover, and cook until melted, about 30 seconds. Serve on rolls with mayonnaise, broccoli rabe, and more red-pepper flakes.

SPICY-SAUSAGE AND LENTIL STEW WITH ESCAROLE SALAD

This Italian-inspired one-pot stew highlights the classic pairing of sausage and lentils, a hearty duo for fall and winter. The simple ingredients simmer together for only about half an hour, then you top them off with escarole—a versatile salad green that's worth getting to know if you're not already a fan. Reheat leftovers over low heat and wait to top the stew with escarole until just before serving.
SERVES 2, WITH LEFTOVERS

---

2 tablespoons extra-virgin olive oil, plus more for drizzling

12 ounces spicy Italian sausage, removed from casing

2 carrots, finely chopped

1 small onion, chopped

4 garlic cloves, minced

Coarse salt and freshly ground pepper

2 tablespoons tomato paste

3 cups low-sodium chicken broth

3 cups water

1 cup brown lentils, rinsed and drained

1 small head escarole, thinly sliced

1 tablespoon fresh lemon juice

1. Heat 1 tablespoon oil in a large pot over medium-high. Add sausage, carrots, onion, and garlic. Season with salt and pepper. Cook, stirring occasionally and breaking up sausage into bite-size pieces, until meat is no longer pink, about 5 minutes. Stir in tomato paste; cook, stirring, 1 minute. Add broth, the water, and lentils. Bring to a boil. Cover, reduce heat to low, and simmer until lentils are tender, about 30 minutes.

2. Meanwhile, toss escarole with lemon juice and remaining tablespoon oil in a large bowl. Season with salt and pepper. Just before serving, top stew with escarole and drizzle with more oil.

SPICY CLAMS WITH SPAGHETTI

If you have a terrific source of fresh shellfish nearby, you'll definitely want to add this super-easy, classic *spaghetti vongole* (pasta with clams) to your weeknight repertoire. Other than the clams, the ingredients are kitchen staples—so you can minimize the shopping next time you're craving a weeknight indulgence. If you like your dish extra spicy, up the amount of red-pepper flakes.
SERVES 2

Coarse salt and freshly ground black pepper

8 ounces spaghetti

2 tablespoons extra-virgin olive oil

2 garlic cloves, minced

¼ teaspoon red-pepper flakes, plus more for serving

¼ cup dry white wine

18 littleneck clams (about 1½ pounds), scrubbed

1 tablespoon unsalted butter

¼ cup fresh flat-leaf parsley leaves, chopped, plus 1 tablespoon thinly sliced stems

1. Bring a pot of generously salted water to a boil. Cook pasta until al dente according to package instructions. Reserve ½ cup pasta water; drain.

2. Meanwhile, heat oil in a large pot over medium. Add garlic and red-pepper flakes, and cook, stirring, 30 seconds. Add wine and bring to a simmer. Raise heat to medium-high and add clams. Cover and cook just until clams open, 4 to 5 minutes. Discard any unopened clams.

3. Stir in butter and parsley leaves and stems. Add pasta and toss to coat, adding reserved pasta water, 1 tablespoon at a time, until sauce is loose and creamy. Season with salt and black pepper.

POACHED SALMON WITH POTATOES, CUCUMBER, AND BUTTERMILK-DILL DRESSING

Add this salmon recipe to your back-pocket dinner shortlist: The technique is straightforward, and the dish strikes that elusive balance of indulgent and virtuous. Poaching the salmon is a cinch, and you can steam the potatoes while the fish cooks. Serve with sliced cucumbers and drizzles of buttermilk-dill dressing for a presentation that feels Scandinavian in its simplicity and wholesomeness. And keep it on hand for dinner parties, too! This is delicious at room temperature, and leftovers make a nice next-day lunch. **SERVES 2, WITH LEFTOVERS**

Coarse salt and freshly ground pepper

1 skin-on salmon fillet (about 1¼ pounds), preferably wild

1 pound baby potatoes, such as Yukon Gold, scrubbed

⅔ cup buttermilk

⅓ cup mayonnaise

3 tablespoons coarsely chopped fresh dill, plus more for serving

1 large cucumber, thinly sliced

Lemon wedges, for serving

1. Bring 1¼ inches of water to a boil in a large straight-sided skillet. Generously season with salt. Add salmon, skin-side down; return to a boil. Remove from heat, cover, and let stand until salmon is just opaque throughout, 15 to 17 minutes. Use a slotted spatula to transfer salmon to a plate, skin-side up.

2. Meanwhile, bring 2 inches of water to a simmer in a large pot fitted with a steamer basket (or a metal colander). Place potatoes in basket, cover, and steam until easily pierced with the tip of a sharp knife, 12 to 15 minutes.

3. Whisk together buttermilk and mayonnaise in a bowl, stir in dill, and season with salt and pepper. Remove skin from salmon; flake fish into large pieces. Divide salmon, potatoes, and cucumber among plates. Drizzle with dressing, sprinkle with dill, and serve with lemon wedges.

BAKED FISH-AND-CHIPS

You probably only have fish-and-chips when you go out to eat, but this recipe proves how fun it can be to try restaurant favorites in your own kitchen. Our version takes a lighter approach to the deep-fried British classic: You bake the fish and potatoes instead of frying them, and use panko to give the cod fillets a nice crunch. To slice the potatoes extra-thin, it's best to use a handheld slicer (or mandoline) instead of a knife. Putting a bottle of malt vinegar on the table will lend an authentic vibe. **SERVES 2**

1   russet potato, scrubbed and cut into very thin slices with a handheld slicer

2   tablespoons extra-virgin olive oil

1   tablespoon fresh rosemary leaves

     Coarse salt and freshly ground pepper

1   cup panko breadcrumbs

¼   cup all-purpose flour

1   large egg

1   pound skinless cod fillet, cut into 1-inch-thick strips

     Lemon wedges, pickles, malt vinegar, ketchup, and flaky sea salt, such as Maldon, for serving (optional)

1. Preheat oven to 400°F with racks in upper and lower thirds. Soak potato in warm water 5 minutes; drain and dry thoroughly. Toss with oil and rosemary, season with salt and pepper, and spread on a rimmed baking sheet. Bake on top rack 20 minutes.

2. Meanwhile, toast panko on another rimmed baking sheet on bottom rack until golden, about 5 minutes. Transfer to a wide dish. Place flour in another dish; season with salt and pepper. Whisk egg in a third dish. Season fish with salt; coat in flour, then egg, then panko. Transfer, narrow-side down, to a parchment-lined baking sheet.

3. Flip potatoes and transfer to lower rack. Place fish on upper rack; bake until fish is just cooked through and potatoes are crisp and golden brown in places, 16 to 18 minutes. Serve with lemon wedges, pickles, vinegar, ketchup, and salt, if desired.

PAPRIKA SHRIMP WITH HUMMUS AND MINT

Adding paprika-spiced shrimp is a simple way to spruce up a humdrum hummus-and-pita supper. Shrimp and hummus complement each other perfectly, and the result is a delicious, speedy, satisfying meal. Just spike the hummus with chopped fresh mint, layer it in a bowl with the shrimp, and serve with warm pita, fresh greens, and sliced radishes and cucumber. **SERVES 2**

2 tablespoons extra-virgin olive oil, plus more for drizzling	1 tablespoon fresh lemon juice, plus wedges for serving
½ pound large shrimp, peeled and deveined	¾ cup plain hummus
2 garlic cloves, minced	1½ tablespoons finely chopped fresh mint, plus sprigs for serving
Coarse salt and freshly ground pepper	Pita bread, warmed, for serving
¼ teaspoon paprika, plus more for sprinkling	Sliced radishes and cucumbers, for serving

1. Heat a large skillet over medium-high. Swirl in 1 tablespoon oil. Add shrimp in a single layer and garlic; season with salt and pepper. Cook, stirring a few times, until shrimp are pink, opaque, and just cooked through, 2 to 3 minutes. Stir in paprika; cook until fragrant, about 30 seconds. Stir in lemon juice, scraping up any browned bits from bottom of pan. Remove from heat.

2. In a bowl, stir together hummus, remaining tablespoon oil, and mint. Serve shrimp and hummus drizzled with oil, sprinkled with paprika, and topped with mint, with lemon wedges, pita, radishes, and cucumbers alongside.

MUSSELS STEAMED WITH GARLIC, TOMATO, AND WHITE WINE

Steaming a pot of mussels is a delicious, no-fuss way to introduce seafood into your weeknight routine, and the end result looks impressive, though mussels actually cook in minutes and are fairly inexpensive. Try this recipe once just for the two of you, and you may start to serve mussels at dinner parties; the quantities multiply easily. Serve with generous amounts of crusty bread, since you'll want to soak up every drop of the broth. **SERVES 2**

2 teaspoons extra-virgin olive oil	¼ cup dry white wine
1 garlic clove, minced	Chopped fresh flat-leaf parsley, for serving
1 small tomato, finely chopped	Crusty bread, for serving
1 pound scrubbed mussels (discard any open ones)	

Heat oil over medium-high in a large pot. Add garlic and cook for 1 minute, then stir in tomato and cook 2 minutes. Add mussels and wine. Cover and cook just until the mussels open (discard any that don't), about 5 minutes. Toss with chopped parsley and serve with crusty bread.

GRILLED SNAPPER SANDWICHES WITH PICKLED VEGETABLES

Reminiscent of Vietnamese–style bánh mì, these phenomenally juicy, crunchy, spicy grilled–snapper sandwiches are topped with Sriracha–spiked mayo and vinegary carrots, cucumbers, and radishes. Make them once, and then the next time the two of you are hosting friends, you'll be able to quickly whip up a big batch. **MAKES 2**

1 carrot, peeled into ribbons	¼ cup mayonnaise
½ small cucumber, such as Persian, thinly sliced	1 teaspoon Sriracha, plus more for serving (optional)
2 radishes, very thinly sliced	1 skinless red-snapper fillet (about 8 ounces)
2 tablespoons unseasoned rice vinegar	Extra-virgin olive oil, for brushing
1 teaspoon sugar	2 Portuguese rolls, halved
Coarse salt and freshly ground pepper	¼ cup lightly packed fresh cilantro leaves

1. Toss carrot, cucumber, radishes, vinegar, sugar, and ¼ teaspoon salt in a bowl. Mix mayonnaise and Sriracha in another bowl.

2. Heat grill (or grill pan) to medium-high (if using a charcoal grill, coals are ready when you can hold your hand 5 inches above grill for just 3 to 4 seconds). Brush fish with oil; season with salt and pepper. Brush grates with oil. Grill fish until bottom edges turn opaque, about 3 minutes. Flip with 2 large spatulas and cook until opaque in center, about 3 minutes more. Remove from grill; cut fillet in half crosswise. Meanwhile, grill rolls until lightly marked.

3. Spread mayonnaise mixture on all roll halves. Layer fish and pickled vegetables on bottom halves; drizzle with pickling liquid and top with cilantro. Serve with more Sriracha, if desired.

FISH STEW WITH HERBED TOASTS

It's hard to believe this incredibly flavorful fish stew comes together in just half an hour with so little work: You simply cook the vegetables, herbs, and fish on the stovetop for a few minutes, then finish the dish in the broiler. Toasted bread brushed with butter and served on the side recalls the much more labor–intensive bouillabaisse. **SERVES 2**

2 tablespoons unsalted butter, room temperature	1/2 can (14.5 ounces) whole peeled plum tomatoes in juice
1 carrot, finely chopped	8 ounces clam juice
1/2 stalk celery, finely chopped	1 pound skinless cod or halibut fillet, cut into 1 1/2-inch pieces
1 shallot, minced	
3 sprigs thyme	2 baguette slices, each cut 1 1/2 inches thick on the diagonal
Coarse salt and freshly ground pepper	

1. Heat broiler with rack 8 inches from the heat source. In a large ovenproof skillet, melt 1 tablespoon butter over medium-high heat. Add carrot, celery, 1 1/2 tablespoons shallot, and 2 thyme sprigs; season with salt. Cook, stirring occasionally, until vegetables are golden in spots, about 5 minutes. Stir in tomatoes and juice; simmer, breaking up tomatoes into bite-size pieces, until liquid is mostly evaporated, about 5 minutes. Stir in clam juice and fish; return to a simmer. Remove from heat.

2. Spread remaining tablespoon butter over bread. Sprinkle with remaining shallot and thyme leaves; season with salt and pepper. Place atop fish. Broil until fish is just cooked through and bread is toasted, about 2 minutes (if bread is darkening too quickly, move skillet to lower rack).

RIGATONI WITH CORN, ARUGULA, AND TUNA

This rigatoni dish is at its best in summer, when fresh corn and in-season tomatoes will bring their intensely sweet, vibrant flavors. Using farm-stand ingredients at the height of deliciousness means you'll hardly need to add much else, but tuna rounds out the dish and gives it a solid hit of protein. Make sure to use tuna packed in olive oil, for the most flavorful results. **SERVES 2**

6	ounces rigatoni	1	tin (5-ounces) tuna in olive oil
	Coarse salt and freshly ground pepper	½	pint cherry or grape tomatoes, halved
2	ears corn, shucked	2	cups baby arugula
3	tablespoons unsalted butter		Lemon wedges, for serving (optional)

1. Cook pasta in a large pot of generously salted boiling water until al dente according to package instructions. Reserve ¼ cup pasta water; drain pasta and return to pot.

2. Meanwhile, slice corn kernels from cobs into a shallow bowl, then scrape corn "milk" from cobs with the side of a spoon into the same bowl. Melt butter in a small saucepan over medium-high. Reduce heat to medium and simmer until butter browns, about 7 minutes. Add corn and corn milk; simmer just until corn is crisp-tender, about 30 seconds.

3. Add corn mixture to pasta with tuna in oil and tomatoes; toss to combine. Season with salt and pepper. Add reserved pasta water, a little at a time, until sauce evenly coats pasta. Let cool 10 minutes. Gently fold in arugula. Serve with lemon wedges, if desired.

FARRO RISOTTO WITH SHRIMP

All you need to make a great risotto is patience, and this farro version is no exception: It requires that you stir the grains constantly in liquid for about half an hour. Add the shrimp and peas for a couple of minutes at the end, and then shower everything with Parmesan and fresh herbs. The result is a comfort-food dish you'll crave all winter. **SERVES 2**

1   cup low-sodium chicken broth

1   cup water

1   tablespoon extra-virgin olive oil

2   scallions, trimmed, white and green parts separated and thinly sliced

¾   cup pearled farro

¼   cup dry white wine

½   pound medium shrimp, peeled and deveined

½   cup frozen peas, thawed

2   tablespoons finely grated Parmigiano-Reggiano, plus more for serving

2   tablespoons finely chopped fresh herbs, such as basil, tarragon, chives, flat-leaf parsley, or chervil, plus more for serving

Coarse salt and freshly ground pepper

1. Bring broth and water to a simmer in a saucepan. In another saucepan, heat oil over medium. Add scallion whites and cook, stirring frequently, until translucent, about 2 minutes. Add farro; cook, stirring constantly, until toasted, about 2 minutes. Add wine and cook, stirring, until absorbed.

2. Add ½ cup broth mixture and cook, stirring, until liquid is absorbed. Continue adding broth in this manner, ¼ cup at a time, until farro is tender but still slightly firm, about 20 minutes. (You may not need all of broth mixture.) Stir in shrimp and peas, and cook until shrimp are opaque, 3 to 4 minutes. Remove from heat; stir in cheese, scallion greens, and chopped herbs. Season with salt and pepper. Divide among bowls, top with chopped herbs, and serve with additional cheese.

SWORDFISH WITH WATERMELON SALAD

Even if you keep watermelon in your fridge all summer, you may not have considered enjoying it on your dinner plate. It actually goes well with many savory ingredients, especially the lime and ginger in the dressing for this salad. Top some watermelon wedges and Bibb lettuce leaves with super-quick grilled swordfish skewers (they cook in just seven minutes). Add chopped scallions, carrots, and the dressing—and prepare to add a whole new dimension to your main-course-salad routine. **SERVES 2**

1½   tablespoons fresh lime juice (from 1 to 2 limes)

1   teaspoon sugar

1   teaspoon finely grated peeled fresh ginger

1½   tablespoons safflower oil, plus more for brushing

Coarse salt and freshly ground pepper

½   pound skinless swordfish steak, cut into 1½-inch pieces

2   large scallions, trimmed, white and pale-green parts separated, dark-green parts thinly sliced

½   head Bibb lettuce, leaves separated

¼   small seedless watermelon, rind removed (if desired), cut into ½-inch-thick wedges

½   carrot, peeled into ribbons and julienned

Flaky sea salt, such as Maldon, for serving

1. For dressing, whisk together lime juice, sugar, ginger, and oil; season with coarse salt.

2. Heat grill (or grill pan) to medium (if using a charcoal grill, coals are ready when you can hold your hand 5 inches above grill for just 3 to 4 seconds). Thread swordfish and scallion whites onto skewers. Brush fish and scallions with oil, and season with salt and pepper. Grill, flipping occasionally, until fish is opaque throughout, about 7 minutes.

3. Divide lettuce and watermelon among plates. Top with skewers. Drizzle with dressing and top with scallion greens and carrot. Sprinkle with sea salt and serve immediately.

TOFU WITH BABY BOK CHOY AND RICE NOODLES

On steamy summer days, the last thing you want to do is stand over a hot stove—but there's only so much salad you can eat. Try this nearly-no-cook recipe for tofu with rice noodles, and chances are you'll find yourself craving it year-round. A quick sauce of vinegar, ginger, soy sauce, honey, and peanut butter brings an intense savory-sweet kick to the tofu, and the noodles are ready after a 10-minute bath in boiling water. (Use hot tap water instead if you really don't want to touch that stove.) **SERVES 4, VERY GENEROUSLY**

1	package (8 ounces) thin rice noodles
1	package (14 ounces) firm tofu, drained
1/3	cup unseasoned rice vinegar
2	teaspoons minced peeled fresh ginger (from a 2-inch piece)
2	tablespoons trimmed and chopped scallions, plus more, sliced, for serving

6	heads baby bok choy (6 ounces), halved
	Coarse salt
1/2	cup low-sodium soy sauce
2	tablespoons honey
1/4	cup chunky or smooth peanut butter
	Chopped peanuts and thinly sliced Thai chiles, for serving

1. Place noodles in a baking dish and cover with very hot tap water. Let stand 10 minutes. Drain; repeat twice more, or until tender.

2. Meanwhile, slice tofu into eight 1/2-inch-thick pieces. Drain on paper towels. Stir together vinegar, ginger, and scallions in a bowl; toss 3 tablespoons of mixture with bok choy in another bowl. Season with salt. Stir soy sauce, honey, and peanut butter into remaining vinegar mixture. Arrange tofu in a single layer in a baking dish; pour soy-sauce mixture over top, turning tofu to coat.

3. Divide noodles, tofu, and bok choy among four serving bowls. Drizzle with soy-sauce mixture. Top with scallions, peanuts, and chiles.

ORECCHIETTE WITH BUTTERNUT SQUASH AND SAGE

This recipe delivers a nice, multi-textured hit of fall flavor, and it's a breeze to pull off. The only time-consuming part is prepping the squash. We love the unexpected mix of ingredients: The dish brings together tender pasta, creamy ricotta (instead of the usual brown butter), and fried sage leaves, a combination inspired by a pumpkin ravioli dish one of our food editors had in Siena, Italy. **SERVES 2**

Coarse salt

6 ounces orecchiette

1 tablespoon extra-virgin olive oil, plus more for drizzling

½ small butternut squash, halved and peeled, seeds and pulp scooped and reserved, flesh cut into ½-inch cubes (2 cups)

1½ tablespoons unsalted butter

2 tablespoons packed fresh sage leaves

⅔ cup whole-milk ricotta cheese, for serving

1. Bring a large pot of generously salted water to a boil. Cook pasta until al dente according to package instructions. Reserve ½ cup pasta water; drain.

2. Meanwhile, heat oil in a large straight-sided skillet over medium. Add squash seeds and pulp. Cook, stirring occasionally, until seeds puff and turn golden, about 10 minutes. Season with salt; transfer to a plate. Add 1 tablespoon butter to skillet; melt. Add sage and cook, stirring occasionally, until crisp, about 2 minutes. Transfer to another plate. Add squash cubes to skillet. Season with salt, cover, and cook, stirring occasionally, until tender, about 10 minutes.

3. Stir in pasta, ¼ cup reserved pasta water, and remaining ½ tablespoon butter. Simmer until thickened slightly, about 2 minutes. Add more pasta water, a few tablespoons at a time, until pasta is evenly coated; season with salt. Divide among bowls and top with squash seeds, sage leaves, and ricotta. Drizzle with oil and serve.

TORTELLINI SOUP WITH PEAS AND SPINACH

When you want to get a cozy, filling dinner on the table in minutes, convenience can be king. You can't go wrong with this tortellini soup, which comes together quickly with a few store–bought ingredients. If that feels like too much of a cheat, by all means use homemade chicken stock if you have some on hand. Either way, this delicious soup will buy the two of you more time to relax over dinner and a glass of wine. **SERVES 2**

---

4   cups low-sodium chicken broth

8   ounces fresh cheese tortellini

½   cup frozen peas

1   cup coarsely chopped baby spinach (about 1 ounce)

Coarse salt and freshly ground pepper

Finely grated Parmigiano-Reggiano, for serving

Lemon wedges, for serving

In a pot, bring broth to a boil over high heat. Add tortellini and cook 2 minutes less than package instructions. Add peas and spinach, and cook until warmed through, 1 to 2 minutes; season with salt and pepper. Serve with Parmesan and lemon wedges.

RICOTTA PIZZA WITH FRESH AND ROASTED TOMATOES

If you've never made pizza at home, it's worth learning how, and this recipe is endlessly adaptable once you've nailed down the method. The crust here is topped with ricotta and Parmesan instead of mozzarella, and it's very simple to make. After the dough bakes in an extra-hot oven, you pile it with a juicy mix of roasted cherry tomatoes and raw in-season tomatoes. **SERVES 4**

1 cup whole-milk ricotta cheese	¼ cup extra-virgin olive oil
1 cup grated Parmigiano-Reggiano (4 ounces)	2 pints cherry or grape tomatoes
Coarse salt and freshly ground pepper	1 large tomato, preferably heirloom, sliced into rounds
1 large egg, lightly beaten	2 tablespoons fresh oregano leaves
1 pound pizza dough, thawed if frozen	

1. Preheat oven to 500°F with racks in upper and lower thirds. Combine ricotta and Parmesan, season with salt and pepper, and stir in egg. On a baking sheet, drizzle pizza dough with 2 tablespoons oil and stretch or roll into a 16-inch-long oval. Spread ricotta mixture on dough, leaving a 1-inch border.

2. On a rimmed baking sheet, toss cherry tomatoes with remaining 2 tablespoons oil and season with salt and pepper. Bake cherry tomatoes on bottom rack and pizza on top rack until tomatoes are soft and skins have burst, about 15 minutes. Remove tomatoes and bake pizza until crust is deep golden brown, about 8 minutes more. Toss cherry tomatoes with sliced tomatoes and oregano; season with salt and pepper. Transfer pizza to a cutting board and top with tomato mixture. Slice and serve immediately.

MINESTRONE WITH WINTER GREENS

Despite its name, this minestrone recipe works anytime you can get your hands on leafy greens like chicory, kale, or escarole (in season well into winter in some regions). Instead of simmering forever on the stove, the soup is ready in less than an hour, thanks to some great flavor shortcuts: caramelizing the tomato paste in a pot with just garlic and oil, then gradually adding the remaining ingredients, and cooking a chunk of pecorino along with the soup as well as grating the cheese on top at the end. **SERVES 2, GENEROUSLY**

¼ cup extra-virgin olive oil, plus more for drizzling	1 large sprig sage
6 garlic cloves, thinly sliced	1 piece (2 ounces) Pecorino Romano, plus more, grated, for serving
1 tablespoon tomato paste	Coarse salt and freshly ground black pepper
2 cans (15.5 ounces each) cannellini beans, rinsed and drained	4 ounces ditalini or other short, tubular pasta (1 cup)
½ cup dry white wine, such as Sauvignon Blanc	4 cups shredded chicory, escarole, or kale
8 cups water	Red-pepper flakes, for serving (optional)

1. Heat a large pot over medium-high. Add oil and garlic; cook, stirring occasionally, until garlic is golden, 2 to 3 minutes. Stir in tomato paste; cook, stirring, 1 minute. Add beans and wine; simmer, stirring occasionally, until liquid has thickened and wine has almost evaporated, about 4 minutes. Add the water, sage, and cheese; season with salt and black pepper. Simmer, partially covered, over medium-low until beans are tender, about 25 minutes.

2. Raise heat and bring soup to a boil, stir in pasta, and cook until al dente according to package instructions, stirring occasionally. Add greens; cook, stirring, just until wilted, about 1 minute. Serve, topped with grated cheese and red-pepper flakes, if desired.

PASTA CAPRESE

When the summer farm stands are spilling over with ripe tomatoes and bunches of fragrant basil, dinner practically makes itself. All you need to do is tear some juicy tomatoes with your hands and toss them in a bowl with prepared pasta, creamy burrata, and a no-cook sauce of olive oil, garlic, salt, and pepper, then top everything with basil. Nothing could be easier or taste more like summer. (Don't bother with this recipe in the winter, though; out-of-season tomatoes aren't nearly flavorful enough to carry the dish.) **SERVES 2**

2 tablespoons extra-virgin olive oil	2 tomatoes
2 garlic cloves, thinly sliced	½ pound burrata or fresh mozzarella cheese
Coarse salt and freshly ground pepper	Fresh basil leaves, for serving
8 ounces short pasta (such as campanelle)	

In a large bowl, combine oil, garlic, ¼ teaspoon salt, and ¼ teaspoon pepper. Meanwhile, cook pasta in a large pot of boiling salted water until al dente according to package instructions. Drain and toss with oil mixture. Tear tomatoes and cheese; scatter over pasta. Garnish with basil leaves and sprinkle with pepper.

Mix-and-Match Mains & Sides

Tried-and-true
recipes for
versatile entrées
and go-with-
anything
accompaniments

CLASSIC ROAST CHICKEN

Five minutes of prep time and an hour of doing next to nothing results in the most satisfying main course, plus plenty of leftovers for salads, sandwiches, and soups. After you've got the basic technique down, experiment with seasoning and aromatics in and around the bird before roasting; we like halved lemons, garlic cloves, shallots or sliced onions, and fresh herbs such as rosemary, thyme, parsley, and oregano. **SERVES 2, WITH LEFTOVERS**

1   whole chicken (3½ to 4 pounds), patted dry

     Coarse salt

     Olive oil (optional)

1. Preheat oven to 450°F. Let chicken stand at room temperature for an hour before roasting. Season chicken generously with salt and set it on a rimmed baking sheet. (If the bird is small, rub with oil for color, but this isn't necessary for one larger than 3½ pounds.) Tie legs firmly together with kitchen twine and tuck wing tips beneath body. Add desired aromatics (see note above).

2. Roast until an instant-read thermometer inserted in a thigh reads 165°F, about 12 minutes per pound. Let chicken rest 10 minutes before carving and serving.

TIP
—

No thermometer? Don't panic. Look for golden skin, legs that feel loose when wiggled, and juices that run clear when you pierce the chicken between the breast and leg with the tip of a knife.

Avocado Citrus Salad

SERVES 2, GENEROUSLY

Remove peel and pith from ½ **grapefruit** and 1 small **navel orange**. Working over a bowl, cut out grapefruit and orange segments, then squeeze juice from membranes. Place 2 cups **baby arugula** on a platter and top with 1 ripe sliced **avocado**, 1 sliced **radish**, and citrus segments with juices. Drizzle with 1 tablespoon **extra-virgin olive oil** and top with 1 thinly sliced **scallion**. Season with **coarse salt** and **freshly ground pepper**, and serve.

Luxurious Mashed Potatoes

SERVES 2

In a large pot, cover 1 pound **Yukon Gold potatoes**, peeled and cut into ½-inch pieces, with **salted water** by 2 inches. Bring to a boil; reduce to a simmer and cook until potatoes are tender, about 12 minutes. Drain thoroughly and pass potatoes through a ricer or food mill into pot. Over low heat, add 4 tablespoons cold **unsalted butter**, cut into pieces, and stir until melted. Continue to cook, stirring constantly, until potatoes are stiff, about 1 minute. Gradually add ¾ cup warmed **heavy cream**, stirring constantly to combine. Using a flexible spatula, pass potatoes through a ricer for a second time or fine-mesh sieve. Season with **coarse salt** and **freshly ground pepper**, and serve immediately.

Brussels Sprouts Slaw

SERVES 2

In a large bowl, whisk together 1½ teaspoons **grainy mustard**, 1 tablespoon plus 1½ teaspoons **white-wine vinegar**, 1 teaspoon **honey**, and 1 tablespoon **extra-virgin olive oil**. Season with **coarse salt** and **freshly ground pepper**. Add ½ pound **brussels sprouts**, trimmed and shredded; ½ small head **radicchio**, cored and thinly sliced; ¼ cup snipped **fresh chives**; and 2 tablespoons toasted **sunflower seeds**. Toss to combine and serve.

Minted Couscous

SERVES 2

In a small saucepan, bring ½ cup **water** to a boil. Remove from heat. Stir in ½ cup **couscous**; season with **coarse salt** and **freshly ground pepper**. Cover and, off heat, let steam in the pan, 5 minutes. Add 2 thinly sliced **scallions**, ¼ cup **fresh mint** leaves, 1½ teaspoons **extra-virgin olive oil**, and 1½ teaspoons **fresh lime juice**; fluff couscous with a fork, and serve.

PAN-FRIED STEAK WITH MUSTARD CREAM SAUCE

Cooking steaks on the stovetop is lightning-fast and efficient. They require only a few minutes in a very hot skillet, which can then be deglazed to make a flavorful sauce. Very little butter is needed to encourage the meat to form a nice crust; be sure to wait until the steaks release easily from the pan before turning them. **SERVES 2**

2	boneless strip steaks (8 to 10 ounces each), 1 inch thick, room temperature
	Coarse salt and freshly ground pepper
2	teaspoons unsalted butter
½	cup vermouth or white wine
2	teaspoons Dijon mustard
¼	cup heavy cream

1. Heat a 10-inch cast-iron skillet over high until very hot but not smoking, about 2 minutes. Season steaks on both sides with salt and pepper. Add half the butter to pan and set one steak directly on top. Repeat with remaining butter and steak. Sear until steaks release easily from pan and a golden brown crust has formed, about 3 minutes. Using tongs, hold steaks and sear outer edges, about 3 seconds each. Turn steaks over and cook until an instant-read thermometer reaches 125°F for medium-rare. Transfer to a warm plate and let rest 5 to 10 minutes.

2. Meanwhile, remove pan from heat and carefully pour in vermouth (it will spatter). Return skillet to heat. Deglaze pan, stirring up browned bits with a wooden spoon; cook until liquid is almost completely reduced, about 45 seconds. Stir in mustard and heat for 15 seconds. Add cream and any juices that have collected on the plate; stir to combine. Cook until sauce lightly coats the back of a spoon, about 10 seconds. Season with salt and pepper. Pour sauce over steaks and serve.

Crushed Peas with Fresh Mint

SERVES 2

Puree 1 tablespoon sliced **fresh basil** and ½ teaspoon finely grated **lemon** zest in a mini chopper or food processor. Add ¼ teaspoon **sugar** and 2 tablespoons lemon juice, and pulse until combined. With machine running, add ¼ cup **extra-virgin olive oil**; season with **coarse salt**. Bring a pot of **water** to a boil. Add 1½ teaspoons salt and 1 cup shelled **fresh garden peas** (from 1 pounds in pods). Reduce heat and vigorously simmer until tender and bright green, about 4 minutes; drain and transfer to a bowl. Add 1 tablespoon basil vinaigrette and partially crush with a potato masher. Season with salt and **freshly ground pepper**, then add 1½ teaspoons thinly sliced **fresh mint**. Drizzle with more vinaigrette, garnish with basil sprigs, and serve.

Honey-Glazed Carrots

SERVES 2

Halve 3 **carrots** lengthwise and cut into 2-inch pieces. In a large skillet, combine carrots and 2 teaspoons **extra-virgin olive oil**; add just enough **water** to cover carrots (about 2 cups). Cook over medium-high heat until water is evaporated and carrots are tender, 15 minutes. Cook, tossing often, until carrots are light golden, about 2 minutes. Add 2 teaspoons **honey**, and 1 tablespoon **dry white wine**, **low-sodium chicken broth**, or water; cook, stirring and scraping up browned bits with a wooden spoon, until carrots are glazed, about 2 minutes. Top with **fresh cilantro** and serve.

Lentil Salad

SERVES 2

Bring a saucepan of water to a boil; add ½ cup **French green lentils**, rinsed and picked over, and 1 **garlic clove**, halved lengthwise. Reduce heat and simmer until lentils are crisp-tender, 10 to 15 minutes. Drain and run lentils under cold water. Discard garlic. In a bowl, toss together lentils, 1 finely chopped large **celery** stalk (about ½ cup), ½ small thinly sliced **red onion** (about ¼ cup), and ½ cup finely chopped **fresh flat-leaf parsley**. In a small bowl, whisk together 3 tablespoons **fresh lemon juice**, 1 tablespoon **extra-virgin olive oil**, and 1 teaspoon **warm water**. Drizzle over lentils and stir gently to incorporate. Season with **coarse salt** and **freshly ground pepper**.

Roasted Cauliflower with Shallots and Golden Raisins

SERVES 2

Preheat oven to 425°F. On a rimmed baking sheet, toss 1 small head **cauliflower**, cut into florets, and 1 large **shallot**, thinly sliced, with 1 tablespoon **extra-virgin olive oil**. Season with **coarse salt** and **freshly ground pepper**. Roast 10 minutes. Meanwhile, in a bowl, whisk together 1 teaspoon **Dijon mustard** and 1½ teaspoons extra-virgin olive oil, then stir in ½ cup **fresh breadcrumbs** and 2 tablespoons **golden raisins**. Sprinkle breadcrumb mixture over cauliflower and roast until breadcrumbs are golden brown and cauliflower is tender, about 10 more minutes. Serve immediately.

FRITTATA

A frittata is great warm or at room temperature, making it a smart option for busy nights when your dinnertimes can vary. The recipe takes well to any combination of vegetables (mushrooms, asparagus, tomatoes, and spinach are all good choices), grated or crumbled cheeses, or cooked meats like crumbled bacon or sliced ham. **SERVES 2**

1	tablespoon unsalted butter
¾	pound potatoes, peeled and cut into 1-inch pieces
2	cups baby kale
6	large eggs
2	tablespoons heavy cream
	Coarse salt and freshly ground pepper

1. Melt butter in a nonstick skillet over medium heat. Add potatoes and cook until golden brown, stirring occasionally, about 20 to 25 minutes. Add kale and cook just until slightly wilted, about 1 minute.

2. Heat broiler. In a bowl, whisk eggs, then whisk in cream. Season with salt and pepper.

3. Pour egg mixture into skillet with kale and potatoes. Cook, using a heatproof flexible spatula to stir and push eggs from edges to center of pan so liquid parts run underneath, until eggs are almost set (they should still be wet on top but set throughout), 2 to 3 minutes.

4. Broil until frittata is set on top and has puffed slightly, 1 to 2 minutes. Gently run the spatula around the edges and underneath the frittata, and carefully slide it out of pan onto a plate. Slice into wedges and serve hot, warm, or at room temperature.

Creamy Baked Acorn Squash

SERVES 2

Preheat oven to 375°F. Halve 1 **acorn squash** (1 pound) lengthwise, then seed and trim "bottom" to lie flat. Place squash, cut-side up, on a rimmed baking sheet and season with **coarse salt** and **freshly ground pepper**. Divide 2 tablespoons **heavy cream** and 4 sprigs **thyme** among halves. Bake until squash is tender when pierced with the tip of a sharp knife, 35 to 40 minutes. Sprinkle with ¼ cup grated **Parmigiano-Reggiano** (1 ounce), and bake until cheese is melted and golden, 10 to 15 minutes more. Serve immediately.

Chile-Garlic Spinach

SERVES 2

In a large skillet, heat 1 teaspoon **safflower oil** over medium-high. Add ½ small thinly sliced **red chile** (such as Fresno or serrano) and 1 small thinly sliced **garlic clove**; cook until fragrant, about 30 seconds. Gradually add 5 cups washed and drained **spinach** and cook, tossing constantly, until wilted, 1 to 2 minutes. Season with **coarse salt**. Serve with **lemon** wedges.

Sautéed Mushrooms

SERVES 2, GENEROUSLY

Heat a large skillet over high. Add 1 tablespoon **extra-virgin olive oil**, swirling to coat. Add ¼ pound cleaned and sliced mixed **mushrooms**, such as chanterelle, cremini, and oyster. Season with a large pinch of **coarse salt** and **freshly ground pepper**, and cook until golden and tender, 4 to 5 minutes. Transfer to a bowl and repeat with another ¼ pound cleaned and sliced mixed mushrooms, using ½ tablespoon extra-virgin olive oil. Add 1 teaspoon **fresh thyme** leaves to second batch, then transfer to bowl. Season with salt and pepper, toss, and serve.

Tomato Salad with Olives and Lemon Zest

SERVES 2

Arrange 1 pound sliced **tomatoes** (any variety) and ¼ cup mixed **olives** on a serving plate. Sprinkle thin strips of **lemon zest** over salad and top with halved **cherry tomatoes**. Drizzle with 1 tablespoon **extra-virgin olive oil**, and season with **coarse salt** and **freshly ground pepper**. Scatter small **fresh basil** leaves over top and serve.

SAUTÉED SOLE

There's no need to fear cooking fish—or reserve it for eating in restaurants. Once you master the simple sauté, you'll always be able to enjoy the catch of the day. This method showcases fish's delicate texture and involves simply cooking it rapidly with a little fat and a few ingredients in a pan over relatively high heat. Flaky, mild-tasting lemon sole works well for this method, or look for flatfish such as flounder; Pacific-caught varieties are the most sustainable. Tilapia works well, too. **SERVES 2**

2 mild skinless white fish fillets (4 to 6 ounces each), such as lemon sole

   Coarse salt and freshly ground pepper

   Wondra flour, for dusting

1½ tablespoons unsalted butter

½ lemon, thinly sliced

Season fish fillets with salt and dust with Wondra flour (we prefer this to all-purpose flour for a lighter texture). Melt butter in a skillet over medium-high heat until foamy. Add fish and cook for 1 minute. Flip, add lemon slices, and cook until fish is opaque, about 1½ minutes. Season fish with salt and pepper, and serve.

Corn and Zucchini Sauté with Basil

SERVES 2

Cut off tips of 3 ears **corn**, husks and silks removed; stand corn upright in a wide, shallow bowl. With a sharp knife, slice downward to release kernels; discard cobs. In a large saucepan, heat 1½ teaspoons **extra-virgin olive oil** over medium-high. Add ½ medium **zucchini**, halved lengthwise and thinly sliced, and 1 small **garlic clove**, minced; cook, tossing, until zucchini is bright green, 1 to 2 minutes. Add corn and season with **coarse salt** and **freshly ground pepper**. Cook, tossing, until corn is heated through, 1 to 3 minutes. Remove from heat, stir in ½ cup **fresh basil** leaves (torn if large) and ½ teaspoon **white-wine vinegar**, and serve.

Roasted Asparagus with Breadcrumbs

SERVES 2, GENEROUSLY

Preheat oven to 425°F. Arrange 1 pound trimmed **asparagus** on a rimmed baking sheet, in a single layer, and drizzle with 1½ teaspoons **extra-virgin olive oil**. Season with ¼ teaspoon **coarse salt** and ⅛ teaspoon **freshly ground pepper**. Roast until tender, 18 to 20 minutes, then transfer to a platter. Meanwhile, melt 1 tablespoon **unsalted butter** in a skillet over medium heat. Add ¼ cup **panko breadcrumbs** and cook, stirring frequently, until deep golden brown, 8 to 10 minutes. Remove from heat and stir in zest and juice from ½ **lemon**. Season with salt. Serve with lemon wedges.

Crisp Potatoes with Rosemary

SERVES 2

Preheat oven to 450°F. In a large pot, cover 1¼ pounds **russet potatoes**, peeled and cut into ¾-inch pieces, with **salted water** by 2 inches. Bring to a boil; reduce to a simmer and cook until potatoes are just tender, about 5 minutes. Drain and immediately toss in a bowl with 2 tablespoons **extra-virgin olive oil** and 1½ teaspoons **fresh rosemary**. (Potatoes will break apart slightly.) Season with **coarse salt** and **freshly ground pepper**. Transfer potatoes to a rimmed baking sheet. Roast, flipping once, until golden and crisp, about 35 minutes. Serve immediately.

Cucumber and Watercress Salad

SERVES 2

In a large bowl, whisk together 1 tablespoon **extra-virgin olive oil**, 1½ tablepoons **white-wine vinegar**, and ½ tablespoon **Dijon mustard**; season with **coarse salt** and **freshly ground pepper**. Add 1 bunch **watercress** (we used Upland cress) and ½ thinly sliced **English cucumber**. Toss to combine and serve.

PAN-FRIED PORK CHOPS

Pork chops are another fast and easy, always reliable supper staple. The key is buying good-quality chops from a butcher or specialty grocery store (look for center-cut chops). They pair well with all kinds of side dishes, especially Luxurious Mashed Potatoes (see page 122). **SERVES 2**

2   bone-in pork chops
(each about 1 inch thick)

Coarse salt and
freshly ground pepper

2   tablespoons unsalted butter

Thyme sprigs

Preheat oven to 400°F. Season pork chops with salt and pepper. Melt butter in an ovenproof skillet over medium-high. Add pork chops and a few sprigs of thyme and sear until chops are golden, 3 to 4 minutes per side. Transfer pork chops in skillet to oven and cook through, about 12 minutes. Serve immediately.

Quinoa-Spinach Pilaf

SERVES 2

In a large saucepan, melt ½ tablespoon **unsalted butter** over medium heat. Add ½ small **yellow onion**, finely chopped, and ½ **garlic clove**, minced; cook until soft, about 4 minutes. Add ½ cup rinsed and drained **quinoa** and cook 1 minute. Add ½ cup plus 2 tablespoons **water** and bring to a boil. Cover, reduce heat, and cook until quinoa is tender but still chewy and has absorbed all the liquid, about 15 minutes. Stir in 2½ cups **baby spinach** and 1½ teaspoons finely grated **lemon zest**; season with **coarse salt** and **freshly ground pepper**, and serve.

Chili-Roasted Sweet Potatoes

SERVES 2

Preheat oven to 425°F. Cut 1 to 2 medium **sweet potatoes** (¾ pound) lengthwise into 8 wedges each. On a large parchment-lined rimmed baking sheet, toss potatoes with 1 tablespoon **extra-virgin olive oil**, 1½ teaspoons **sugar**, ½ teaspoon **chili powder**, ½ teaspoon **coarse salt**, and ⅛ teaspoon **freshly ground pepper** until coated. Arrange wedges cut-sides down. Roast sweet potatoes until browned and tender, 15 to 20 minutes. Season with additional salt, if desired, and serve.

Roasted Beets with Yogurt Sauce

SERVES 2

Preheat oven to 425°F. In a 9-by-13-inch baking dish, toss 1½ bunches **baby beets** or ½ bunch medium beets (about ¾ pound total), scrubbed, with 1½ teaspoons **extra-virgin olive oil**. Season with **coarse salt** and **freshly ground pepper**. Cover dish tightly with foil and roast until tender when pierced with a knife, about 45 minutes (depending on size). When cool enough to handle, rub beets with a paper towel to remove skins.

Meanwhile, in a small bowl, whisk together ¼ cup **plain yogurt**, pinch of **ground cumin**, and 1½ teaspoons fresh **lemon** juice; season with salt and pepper. Spoon yogurt sauce alongside beets, sprinkle with chopped **fresh dill**, and serve with lemon wedges.

Lemony Braised Broccoli

SERVES 2

In a large skillet, heat ½ tablespoon **extra-virgin olive oil** over medium-high. Add ½ medium **yellow onion**, cut into 1-inch wedges; sauté until golden, about 6 minutes. Add 1 smashed **garlic clove**, ½ teaspoon **ground coriander**, and ⅛ teaspoon **red-pepper flakes**; cook until fragrant, about 30 seconds. Add 1 small bunch **broccoli**, cut into florets, stalks peeled and thinly sliced; 1 tablespoon thin **lemon**-zest strips; and 1 cup water. Bring to a boil, then reduce heat and cover. Cook until fork-tender, about 8 minutes. Season with **coarse salt** and red-pepper flakes, and serve with lemon wedges.

CHICKEN PAILLARDS

The French term *paillard* may sound fancy, but it just refers to flattened meat (usually chicken, pork, or veal). You can find thin cutlets at some grocery stores, but you will save money by buying larger pieces and pounding them yourself. First, place a boneless, skinless chicken breast half between two squares of plastic wrap. Using a meat pounder or the bottom of a saucepan, pound chicken evenly until just more than ¼ inch thick. **SERVES 2**

2	chicken paillards (from 1 breast half)
	Coarse salt and freshly ground pepper
1½	teaspoons extra-virgin olive oil, plus more as needed
2	tablespoons cold unsalted butter
2	tablespoons minced shallot
	Juice of 1 lemon (reserve halves)
¼	cup plus 2 tablespoons low-sodium chicken broth
1	tablespoon chopped fresh flat-leaf parsley

1. Season chicken on both sides with salt and pepper. Heat oil and about ½ tablespoon butter in a large skillet over medium-high until butter melts and foams. Add paillards and sauté on one side until golden brown, about 2 minutes. Reduce heat to medium, flip paillards, and sauté until cooked through, about 2 minutes. Transfer to a plate.

2. Add shallot to skillet and cook over medium heat, adding oil as needed, stirring often, until golden, about 1 minute. Raise heat to medium-high. Add lemon juice and reserved halves, broth, and any plate juices, and deglaze pan, scraping brown bits from bottom with a wooden spoon. Simmer until sauce reduces by half, about 2 minutes. Gradually stir in remaining butter (in pieces) until just melted and top with parsley. Season with salt and pepper.

Iceberg Wedges with Tahini Dressing

SERVES 2

In a food processor, puree ¼ cup **tahini**, grated zest and juice of ½ **lemon**, 1½ teaspoons **extra-virgin olive oil**, 1 chopped small **garlic clove**, ¼ teaspoon **ground cumin**, ¼ teaspoon **paprika**, and ½ cup plus 2 tablespoons **water** until smooth. Season with **coarse salt**. Core ½ head **iceberg lettuce** and cut into 4 wedges. Drizzle dressing over top of wedges. Sprinkle with chopped **pistachios**, **freshly ground pepper**, and **microgreens** or fresh herbs, and serve.

Polenta with Pecorino

SERVES 2

In a large saucepan, combine 2 cups **water**, ½ teaspoon **coarse salt**, and ⅛ teaspoon **freshly ground pepper**; bring to a boil. Whisking constantly, gradually add ¼ cup plus 2 tablespoons **yellow cornmeal** (not fine ground). Reduce heat to medium-low; cook, whisking often, until thickened, 10 to 15 minutes. Remove from heat and stir in ¼ cup finely grated **Pecorino Romano cheese** (1 ounce) and 2 teaspoons **unsalted butter**. Serve immediately, sprinkled with more cheese and pepper.

Green Beans with Lime and Mint

SERVES 2

In a large pot of boiling **salted water**, cook ½ pound trimmed **green beans** until crisp-tender, about 3 minutes; drain and rinse under cold water. Transfer to a bowl and toss with ½ teaspoon **extra-virgin olive oil, mint** sprigs or 1 tablespoon plus 1½ teaspoons chopped fresh mint leaves, and ½ teaspoon fresh **lime juice,** or to taste. Season with **coarse salt** and **freshly ground pepper**, and serve.

Dijon Potato Salad

SERVES 2

Set a steamer basket in a saucepan with 2 inches simmering water. Add ¾ pound **red new potatoes**, scrubbed and halved (quartered if large). Cover and steam just until tender, 15 to 20 minutes. In a serving bowl, combine 1½ teaspoons **white-wine vinegar** and 1½ teaspoons **Dijon mustard**; season with **coarse salt** and **freshly ground pepper**. Add potatoes and toss; let cool, tossing occasionally. Add 1 tablespoon **extra-virgin olive oil** and ¼ cup chopped **fresh flat-leaf parsley** to potatoes. Season with salt and pepper, toss, and serve.

CAESAR SALAD

Think of this as the perfect dinner when you're looking for something light and crunchy that won't weigh you down. You'll see how easy it is to make the dressing from scratch and how much better it tastes than using store-bought. If you prefer not to use the raw yolk in this recipe, substitute 1 tablespoon of mayonnaise. **SERVES 2**

½   rustic Italian loaf, cut into cubes

2   tablespoons unsalted butter, melted

1   garlic clove, minced

4   anchovy fillets

    Coarse salt and freshly ground pepper

1   tablespoon fresh lemon juice

1   teaspoon Worcestershire sauce

½   teaspoon Dijon mustard

1   large egg yolk, preferably organic

⅓   cup extra-virgin olive oil

1   head romaine lettuce, outer leaves discarded, inner leaves washed and dried

½   cup finely grated Parmigiano-Reggiano, plus more for serving

1. Preheat oven to 450°F. Toss bread cubes with butter and spread in a single layer on a rimmed baking sheet. Bake until cubes are golden, about 10 minutes.

2. In a bowl, mash garlic, anchovies, and 1 teaspoon salt into a paste using two forks. Transfer garlic mixture to a clean jar with a tight-fitting lid. Add 1 teaspoon pepper, the lemon juice, Worcestershire sauce, mustard, egg yolk, and olive oil. Screw the lid on the jar tightly and shake to combine. (Dressing can be refrigerated up to 4 days; shake jar before each use.)

3. Chop or tear lettuce into 1- to 1½-inch pieces, and place in a salad bowl. Add croutons, cheese, and about half the dressing, tossing well with tongs. Shave more cheese over top and serve immediately.

Dessert

Simple-to-follow
recipes for sweet
treats to make
and to share

WARM CHOCOLATE PUDDING CAKES

There's something extra-special about an individually sized dessert—especially when it's a molten chocolate cake served warm out of the oven. You can prepare these rich chocolate pudding cakes up to a day ahead and refrigerate them, then just pop them in the oven when you sit down to dinner. They'll be done by the time you're ready for dessert. And they reheat easily, so you can have two one night and two the next. **MAKES 4**

---

4 ounces semisweet or bittersweet chocolate, chopped

4 tablespoons unsalted butter

¼ cup sugar

2 large eggs, separated

½ teaspoon pure vanilla extract

¼ teaspoon salt

Ice cream, for serving (optional)

1. Preheat oven to 375°F. Place four 6- to 8-ounce ovenproof bowls on a rimmed baking sheet.

2. Place chocolate and butter in a heatproof bowl set over (not in) a saucepan of gently simmering water. Stir occasionally just until melted, 4 to 5 minutes. Remove from heat; mix in 2 tablespoons sugar, then egg yolks and vanilla.

3. In a medium bowl, with an electric mixer, beat egg whites and salt until soft peaks form. With mixer running, gradually add remaining 2 tablespoons sugar; beat until mixture is stiff and glossy.

4. Using a flexible spatula, fold about a third of egg-white mixture into chocolate mixture; gently fold in remaining egg-white mixture just until combined. Divide among bowls. (Puddings can be prepared in advance up to this point; cover with plastic wrap and refrigerate up to 1 day.)

5. Bake until tops are puffed and cracked but insides are still quite soft (a toothpick inserted in center will come out gooey), 20 to 25 minutes (or 25 to 30 minutes if refrigerated). Serve warm or at room temperature (puddings will sink as they cool), topped with ice cream, if desired.

CHOCOLATE CHIP COOKIES

You've no doubt made chocolate chip cookies before and tried several recipes. But have you found the one you're ready to commit to for life? The search is over: This one is a keeper. Simple and straightforward, it's also brilliantly engineered to produce crispy-edged, soft-in-the-middle, all-around-perfect cookies. Make these a few times, memorize the recipe, and it may very well become the dessert you can whip up anytime you have friends over—or just want to treat yourselves. **MAKES 20**

2¾	cups all-purpose flour	1¼	cups packed dark-brown sugar
1¼	teaspoons salt	¾	cup granulated sugar
1	teaspoon baking powder	2	large eggs
1	teaspoon baking soda	1	teaspoon pure vanilla extract
1¼	cups (2½ sticks) unsalted butter, room temperature	1½	cups semisweet chocolate chips

1. Sift together flour, salt, baking powder, and baking soda into a medium bowl.

2. Preheat oven to 350°F. Beat butter and both sugars with a mixer on medium-high speed until pale and fluffy, about 4 minutes. Beat in eggs 1 at a time. Add vanilla. Reduce speed to low. Add flour mixture; beat until combined. Fold in chocolate chips.

3. Using a 2¼-inch ice cream scoop (about 3 tablespoons), drop dough onto parchment-lined baking sheets, spacing about 2 inches apart. Bake until golden around edges but soft in the middle, about 15 minutes. Transfer sheets to a wire rack; let cookies cool 5 minutes. Transfer cookies to rack and let cool completely.

RHUBARB-RASPBERRY GALETTES

Making pie from scratch is not an everyday activity, but if you plan ahead and have a round of dough in your refrigerator, you can prepare these free-form pastries in a flash. Strawberry-rhubarb is a better known combination, but we prefer raspberries as a partner to the tart stalks. **MAKES 4**

½ recipe Pie Dough (page 283)	2 tablespoons cornstarch
All-purpose flour, for surface	1 cup granulated sugar
¾ pound trimmed rhubarb, cut into ¼-inch pieces (about 2½ cups)	Coarse sanding sugar, for sprinkling
4 ounces fresh raspberries (about ¾ cup)	

1. Divide dough evenly into 4 pieces. On a lightly floured surface, roll out each piece to a 7-inch round about ⅛ inch thick. Transfer rounds to large parchment-lined rimmed baking sheets, arranging them several inches apart. (If rounds become too soft to handle, refrigerate until firm, about 20 minutes.)

2. In a large bowl, toss rhubarb, raspberries, cornstarch, and granulated sugar. Cover each round of dough with a heaping ½ cup rhubarb mixture, leaving a 1-inch border. Fold edges over rhubarb filling, leaving an opening in center; gently brush water between folds and press gently so that folds adhere. Refrigerate or freeze until firm, about 30 minutes.

3. Preheat oven to 400°F. Brush edges of dough with water and sprinkle with sanding sugar. Bake until crusts are golden brown, rotating sheets halfway through, about 30 minutes. Reduce heat to 375°F, and bake until juices bubble and start to run out from center of each galette, about 15 minutes more. Transfer to a wire rack and let cool completely before serving.

CLASSIC SHORTBREAD

This simple yet intensely rich shortbread is fantastic on its own, but it practically begs to be served with nearly any sweet sidekick (ice cream, lemon curd, caramel sauce) or dipped in melted chocolate. Even better, you can try a different topping every day, since the shortbread keeps for up to two weeks. All you'll need to make it are flour, salt, butter, and confectioners' sugar; because those four ingredients play a starring role, quality is key. Try baking with high-grade butter, for instance, and note the difference. It's a lesson in how the quality of the ingredients you choose can impact your results. **MAKES 8**

1   cup (2 sticks) unsalted butter, room temperature, plus more for pan

2   cups all-purpose flour

1¼ teaspoons coarse salt

¾   cup confectioners' sugar

1. Preheat oven to 300°F. Butter a 10-inch fluted tart pan with a removable bottom.

2. Sift flour and salt into a bowl. With an electric mixer, beat butter on medium-high speed until fluffy, 3 to 5 minutes, scraping down sides of bowl as needed. Gradually add confectioners' sugar; beat until pale and fluffy, about 2 minutes. Reduce speed to low. Add flour mixture all at once; mix until just combined.

3. Using plastic wrap, press dough into prepared pan. With plastic on dough, refrigerate 20 minutes. Remove plastic wrap. Cut dough into 8 wedges with a paring knife or bench scraper.

4. Bake until golden brown and firm in center, about 1 hour. Transfer pan to a wire rack. Recut shortbread into wedges; let cool completely in pan. (Cookies can be stored in an airtight container at room temperature up to 2 weeks.)

LEMON CUSTARD CAKES

When you want a break from chocolate (okay, maybe that doesn't happen too often), these exquisite little cakes make an intensely satisfying dessert. The recipe needs no special ingredients. Simply mix the batter, pour into custard cups (or ramekins), and bake. About 20 minutes later, you'll have a half-dozen light, springy, tart-and-sweet cakes—puffy on top with a pudding-like texture on the bottom. Add a light dusting of confectioners' sugar, and they're ready for a dressy dinner party or a relaxed afternoon tea. **MAKES 6**

Unsalted butter, room temperature, for cups

3 large eggs, separated

½ cup granulated sugar

2 tablespoons all-purpose flour

3 teaspoons finely grated lemon zest, plus ¼ cup fresh lemon juice (from 2 to 3 lemons)

1 cup milk

¼ teaspoon salt

Confectioners' sugar, for dusting

1. Preheat oven to 350°F. Bring water to boil. Line a large roasting pan or baking dish with a clean kitchen towel. Butter six 6-ounce custard cups and place in prepared pan or dish.

2. In a large bowl, whisk egg yolks and sugar until light; whisk in flour. Gradually whisk in lemon juice, then milk and zest.

3. With an electric mixer, beat egg whites and salt until soft peaks form. Add to lemon batter and fold in gently with a whisk (batter will be quite liquidy).

4. Divide batter among prepared cups; place prepared pan or dish in oven and carefully fill with boiling water to reach halfway up sides of cups. Bake until custards are puffed and lightly browned, 20 to 25 minutes. Transfer to a wire rack to cool. Serve slightly warm or at room temperature, dusted with confectioners' sugar.

BLACKBERRY CRUMBLE

Master this crumble recipe and you'll never again wonder what to do with all the gorgeous seasonal fruit you find at the market (besides eating it raw). This version calls for berries, but substitute other fruits like apples or peaches (chop them first, to about the size of blackberries) as you wish. You can bake the crumble in one dish or in individual ramekins. Either way, stick to the method described in this recipe and sprinkle with the same topping. The dessert is best eaten soon after it comes out of the oven—browned, fragrant, and bubbling with fruit juices—with ice cream scooped on top. **SERVES 4**

4 cups fresh blackberries (about 1 pound)	¼ teaspoon ground cinnamon
¼ cup plus 1 tablespoon sugar	Pinch of salt
3 tablespoons all-purpose flour	6 store-bought sugar cookies (about 2 ounces), coarsely crushed
3 tablespoons fresh lemon juice	
3 tablespoons unsalted butter, room temperature, plus more for dish	¼ cup old-fashioned rolled oats
	Ice cream, for serving (optional)

1. Preheat oven to 375°F. Stir blackberries, ¼ cup sugar, 2 tablespoons plus 1½ teaspoons flour, and lemon juice in a bowl.

2. In a small bowl, stir butter, cinnamon, salt, and remaining tablespoon sugar vigorously with a flexible spatula until creamy. Stir in cookies, oats, and remaining 1½ teaspoons flour. Work mixture through fingers until it forms coarse crumbs, ranging in size from peas to gum balls.

3. Butter a 1½-quart baking dish. Pour blackberry mixture into dish and transfer it to a rimmed baking sheet. Sprinkle mixture with crumb topping. Bake until juices are bubbling and topping is golden brown, 25 to 30 minutes. Let cool on a rack 20 minutes before serving with ice cream, if desired.

PEACH SHORTCAKE

Strawberry shortcake deserves its place in the dessert hall of fame, but you don't need berries to make a wonderful shortcake. This one is made with juicy peak-of-season peaches, sprinkled with fruit brandy, layered on easy buttermilk biscuits, and topped with whipped cream. You can substitute other fruits, but if you choose peaches, make sure they are fragrant; if they don't smell like peaches, they aren't likely to taste like them. And feel free to halve the filling amounts if it's just the two of you. The biscuits are best eaten the same day, though they freeze well; reheat for 10 to 15 minutes in a 300°F oven just before serving. **SERVES 4 (MAKES 9 BISCUITS)**

4	ripe peaches, sliced	¾	teaspoon salt
1	tablespoon kirsch	½	teaspoon baking soda
1	tablespoon sugar, plus more for sprinkling tops	6	tablespoons cold unsalted butter, cut into pieces
2¼	cups all-purpose flour, plus more for dusting	1	cup buttermilk
2¼	teaspoons baking powder	1	cup heavy cream
		½	teaspoon pure vanilla extract

1. Preheat oven to 450°F. Toss peaches with kirsch and sugar. Whisk flour, baking powder, salt, and baking soda in another bowl. With a pastry blender, work in butter until mixture resembles coarse meal. With a fork, mix in buttermilk until just combined. Turn out mixture onto a lightly floured work surface. With floured hands, quickly pat dough into a 9-inch square, about 1 inch thick. Using a floured bench scraper or knife, cut into 9 (3-inch) squares.

2. Arrange squares on a parchment-lined baking sheet. Sprinkle with sugar. Bake until golden brown, about 15 minutes. Transfer to a wire rack to cool completely.

3. In a large bowl, beat cream and vanilla until stiff peaks form. Split biscuits and sandwich with peaches and cream.

DOUBLE CHOCOLATE BROWNIES

The best brownies need absolutely no special ingredients or decorations—
no chocolate chips, no M&Ms, no frosting, nothing. Their magic lies in a subtly
crisp crust and a fudgy, moist (but not too gooey) middle. To that end, this recipe
calls for bittersweet chocolate as well as cocoa powder. With just the seven
ingredients here, you'll turn out the most crowd-pleasing brownies. Feel
free to mix ½ cup coarsely chopped walnuts or pecans into the batter at
the end of step 1. **MAKES 16**

½	cup (1 stick) unsalted butter, cut into large pieces
6	ounces bittersweet chocolate, chopped
1½	cups sugar
3	large eggs

¼	cup unsweetened cocoa powder
½	teaspoon coarse salt
½	cup plus 2 tablespoons all-purpose flour

1. Preheat oven to 350°F. Line an 8-inch square baking pan with parchment, leaving a slight
overhang on all sides. Melt butter and chocolate in a heatproof bowl set over a pot of simmering
water, stirring until smooth. Remove from heat and whisk in sugar. Whisk in eggs, 1 at a time,
until combined. Whisk in cocoa and salt. Fold in flour until just combined.

2. Pour batter into prepared pan, smoothing top with an offset spatula. Bake until set and a
toothpick inserted into the center comes out with moist crumbs, 35 to 40 minutes, rotating pan
halfway through. Let cool slightly in pan, about 15 minutes. Lift brownies from pan using
parchment. Transfer to a wire rack. Let cool completely. Cut into 16 squares. (Brownies can be
stored in an airtight container at room temperature for up to 3 days.)

miss you

BROILED PLUMS

Sometimes all you want after dinner is a bowl of fruit. With a little brandy and a sprinkle of light-brown sugar, fresh plums can be transformed into a warm, juicy, caramelized dessert. Whether you serve the broiled fruit as is or top it with mascarpone, whipped cream, ice cream, or frozen yogurt, the plums cap off the evening on a deliciously sweet and not-too-heavy note. Feel free to substitute any juicy fruit you have around—apricots, peaches, figs, or, for a tarter flavor, red plums instead of black. Just make sure the fruit you choose is ripe but not too soft to the touch; it should yield to gentle pressure. **SERVES 2**

6   Italian prune plums, halved and pitted

3   tablespoons brandy

¼   cup packed light-brown sugar

Heat broiler with rack 6 inches from the heat source. Place plum halves, cut-sides up, in a single layer in an 8-inch square baking pan. Pour brandy evenly over plums and sprinkle with sugar. Broil until plums are soft and sugar is caramelized, 8 to 10 minutes.

PERFECT POUND CAKE

As long as you have the basic refrigerator and pantry staples on hand, you can whip up this buttery-sweet classic. This recipe even skips leaveners like baking soda and baking powder; instead, you give the cake its requisite lift by beating the butter, cream cheese, and sugar until fluffy. The endlessly adaptable cake is lovely with a simple lemon glaze (2 cups confectioners' sugar whisked with ¼ cup fresh lemon juice until smooth), or you can serve it with fresh or roasted fruits, lemon curd, chocolate sauce, or ice cream. It goes without saying that it's heavenly on its own, too. **MAKES TWO 9-BY-5-INCH CAKES**

Vegetable oil cooking spray

3 cups all-purpose flour

2 teaspoons salt

1½ cups (3 sticks) unsalted butter, room temperature

8 ounces (1 bar) cream cheese, room temperature

3 cups sugar

6 large eggs

1 teaspoon pure vanilla extract

Lemon glaze (optional; see note above)

1. Preheat oven to 350°F. Generously coat two 9-by-5-inch loaf pans with cooking spray. In a bowl, whisk together flour and salt.

2. With an electric mixer on high, beat butter and cream cheese until smooth. Gradually add sugar, beating until pale and fluffy, about 5 minutes. Add eggs, 1 at a time, beating well after each. Mix in vanilla. With mixer on low; add flour mixture in 2 batches, beating until just combined.

3. Divide batter between prepared pans. Tap pans on counter; smooth tops with an offset spatula. Bake until golden and a cake tester comes out with a few crumbs attached, 70 to 85 minutes (tent with foil if tops brown too quickly). Transfer pans to a wire rack to cool 10 minutes. Turn out onto rack to cool completely, about 2 hours. (Cake can be stored wrapped in plastic at room temperature, up to 3 days. Or wrap in plastic and freeze up to 3 weeks; thaw, wrapped, at room temperature.) Set rack over a parchment-lined baking sheet. Pour lemon glaze, if using, over cakes, letting it drip down sides. Let set, about 30 minutes before serving.

ESPRESSO GRANITA

If you can make coffee, you can master this simple but sophisticated dessert. You just add sugar to espresso (decaf works, too) and chill it in a bowl, then freeze it for two hours until all the liquid turns into ice crystals. As the granita freezes, remember to stir it with a fork every half hour. Serve this light, refreshing dessert with a dollop of whipped cream, and add a sprinkle of ground espresso and a biscotti on the side, if you'd like. **SERVES 2**

2 cups hot freshly brewed espresso

½ cup sugar

½ cup heavy cream

1 teaspoon finely ground espresso beans (optional)

1. Prepare an ice-water bath. Put espresso and sugar into a medium glass bowl; stir until sugar has dissolved. Set in ice-water bath; stir until cooled.

2. Transfer mixture to a 9-by-13-inch glass baking dish; place in freezer. Chill until mixture begins to solidify, about 45 minutes. Remove from freezer; stir with a fork until mixture begins to break up. Freeze, scraping with fork every 30 minutes, until completely frozen and fine crystals form, about 2 hours total.

3. Whisk cream in a chilled bowl until soft peaks form. Serve granita in glasses or bowls, dolloped with whipped cream and sprinkled with ground espresso, if desired.

CARAMEL POTS DE CRÈME

Pots de crème are essentially just puddings, despite the fancy-sounding French name. Rich, elegant, and luxuriously creamy, they make a showstopping date-night dessert (the recipe makes six, so you'll have some left over). Don't let the recipe intimidate you: It's super-straightforward if you follow it step by step. Just make sure you don't overcook the custard—it should wiggle only slightly when you take the ramekins out of the oven. **MAKES 6**

¾	cup sugar	1	vanilla bean, split
1	cup milk	5	large egg yolks
1½	cups heavy cream	¼	teaspoon salt

1. Preheat oven to 300°F. Place six 4-ounce ovenproof ramekins or custard cups in a large roasting pan. Place ½ cup sugar in a saucepan set over medium heat. Cook, without stirring, until sugar has caramelized and is golden brown, about 3 minutes. Swirl pan, dissolving unmelted sugar, and reduce heat to low. Slowly and carefully whisk in milk and 1 cup cream. Scrape vanilla seeds into pan and add pod. Raise heat to medium-high and bring to a boil; remove pan from heat.

2. In a bowl, whisk together remaining ¼ cup sugar, egg yolks, and salt until pale yellow in color. Slowly add hot cream mixture, whisking constantly; pour through a fine sieve set over a large liquid-measuring cup, discarding vanilla pod. Skim surface to remove any air bubbles. Divide custard evenly among ramekins. Carefully fill roasting pan with hot water to within 1 inch of ramekin tops. Cover with foil and poke small holes in two opposite corners to allow steam to vent. Carefully place pan on center oven rack; bake until just set, about 35 minutes. Remove foil and transfer ramekins to a wire rack to cool completely. Cover with plastic wrap and refrigerate until cold, at least 2 hours and up to 2 days. Whisk remaining ½ cup cream in a chilled mixing bowl just until soft peaks form. Top each serving with whipped cream.

APPLE TART

When you're craving a warm, buttery fruit dessert but can't spend all afternoon making a double-crust pie, this tart should hit the spot. One tip to note: When brushing the pastry with egg wash, don't let it drip over the edges, since the dough will stick to the pan and won't rise properly. You'll want to keep puff pastry in your freezer and a jar of apple jelly or apricot jam around, so you can make this tart anytime the mood strikes. **SERVES 4 TO 6**

1	sheet frozen puff pastry (from a 17.3-ounce package), thawed
	All-purpose flour, for surface
3	Granny Smith apples
⅓	cup sugar

1	large egg yolk beaten with 1 teaspoon water, for egg wash
2	tablespoons unsalted butter
2	tablespoons apple jelly or apricot jam
1	tablespoon water

1. Preheat oven to 375°F. Open pastry sheet and remove paper. Fold sheet back up. On a lightly floured work surface, roll out folded pastry sheet to an 8-by-14-inch rectangle. Trim edges with a pizza cutter or sharp paring knife. Transfer to a rimmed baking sheet and chill in freezer. Meanwhile, peel, core, and slice apples ¼ inch thick. Toss in a large bowl with sugar.

2. Use a sharp paring knife to score a ¾-inch border around pastry (do not cut all the way through). Brush border with egg wash, avoiding edges. Arrange apples inside border and dot with butter. Bake until pastry is golden and apples are tender, 30 to 35 minutes.

3. Heat jelly with the water until melted. Brush apples with glaze. Let cool 15 minutes. Serve warm or at room temperature.

TARTUFO FOR TWO

Even if you make this gorgeous Italian frozen dessert using store-bought ice cream and cookies, you still get to take all the credit. While extremely easy to assemble, the tartufo requires just enough attention to qualify as a special-occasion treat. Choose two ice cream flavors that go together (chocolate and pistachio is our favorite combination, but simply a suggestion). **SERVES 2**

½ cup chocolate ice cream	5 chocolate wafer cookies, pulsed to fine crumbs in a food processor
½ cup pistachio ice cream	2½ teaspoons coconut oil, melted
2 maraschino cherries	2 ounces chopped dark chocolate

1. Line a 4½-inch-diameter glass bowl (with 1⅓ cups capacity) with plastic wrap, leaving an overhang around edges. Pack chocolate ice cream into one half of the bowl; pack pistachio ice cream into other half. Make 2 indentations, about 1 inch deep, in the ice cream, and put 1 cherry in each indentation. Cover the cherries with ice cream; smooth surface. Cover with plastic wrap overhang. Freeze until firm, 2 hours, or up to overnight.

2. In a small bowl, combine cookie crumbs and 1 teaspoon coconut oil. Remove plastic wrap from top of bowl. Press cookie crumbs on top of ice cream. Use an offset spatula to flatten and smooth the top. Re-cover with plastic wrap. Freeze until firm, at least 15 minutes.

3. Melt chocolate in a small heatproof bowl set over (not in) a pan of simmering water (or in the microwave). Stir in remaining 1½ teaspoons coconut oil.

4. Remove top layer of wrap from bowl. Invert bowl onto a wire rack over a rimmed baking sheet. Use a hot wet cloth to wipe the outside of the bowl and loosen the ice cream. Lift bowl and remove plastic wrap. Pour chocolate on top in one continuous stream for the smoothest surface, starting in the center and working your way outward and around.

5. Transfer tartufo on the rack to the freezer to harden the chocolate shell, at least 5 minutes. Remove tartufo from wire rack to a plate using a thin metal spatula that has been dipped in hot water and wiped dry. Serve immediately.

PART THREE

GATHER
ROUND

———

Sharing great food and drinks with friends and family is the natural next step after learning to cook with and for each other. Yet the planning, prepping, and cooking that are built into hosting a group can feel more fraught than festive, whether it's new to you or old hat. The best strategy? Play to your individual strengths. One of you may be a master list maker and bartender, the other a great baker who can also style a dreamy tablescape. Divide and conquer, then kick back and relax.

Page through the following twelve menus, all loosely organized to represent a year's worth of gatherings. See what appeals to you and what suits the occasion (even if there's no occasion at all—sometimes a delicious-sounding meal is the only excuse you need). Among them are an easy, help-yourself brunch; a stylish, New Year's Eve–worthy cocktail party; a midsummer night's dream of a dinner; and a homey Thanksgiving feast with all the trimmings. As for recipes, there's a mix of classic crowd-pleasers and more of-the-moment menu items—cocktails like manhattans and margaritas along with beet-and-lemon shrubs and Aperol spritzes. There's Spanish paella and a Mediterranean grilled leg of lamb marinated with preserved lemon and herbs. And the desserts include Texas-size sheet cake, ice-cream pretzel pie, and mini cheesecakes topped with apricot jam.

Like the everyday recipes in Part Two, these dishes bolster your collective cooking know-how as you try them. Ingredients, equipment, techniques, and new flavors are introduced, explored, and explained. Never set up a buffet table before? How about a grill? Do you know which caviar to buy, and why? Don't stress. The answers are here for you.

The less you have to do on the day you're hosting, the more you can chill, so there's a pre-party prep plan and make-ahead tips for each menu. And keep in mind that the menus are meant to be customized to your liking. For example, if you're looking for cocktail recipes without the finger foods, or you're making a pasta dinner but someone else is bringing dessert, just pick and choose from the suggestions here. The recipes also give you great go-to ideas for when you're on the other end of an invitation—looking for a pie to bake and tote along to Friendsgiving, say, or putting together a meze platter to pack for a picnic.

GAME DAY CHILI

If you're new to hosting a crowd, this carefree menu is for you. Chili practically defines party food: It's simple to pull off, a little goes a long way, and it tastes better when made a day or two ahead. It's as easy to eat while standing as it is while sitting down—like the best guests, it's versatile, adaptable, and welcome in (nearly) any setting. **SERVES 8**

The Menu Eight-Layer Dip ▪ Watercress Salad with Pepitas ▪ Hearty Beef Chili ▪ Vegetarian Green Chili ▪ Skillet Cornbread ▪ Texas Sheet Cake

Eight-Layer Dip

This starter is an all-around, all-time, crowd-pleasing party favorite if ever there was one. It's especially delicious with freshly refried beans, so if you have the time (about 15 minutes), heat and mash them yourself.

- 2 cups Refried Beans (recipe follows) or 1 can (16 ounces)
- 2 teaspoons fresh lime juice
- 2 tablespoons water
  Coarse salt and freshly ground pepper
- ½ cup sour cream
- ½ cup grated cheddar cheese (2 ounces)
- 1 can (4.5 ounces) chopped green chiles
- 2 tomatoes, chopped
- 1 ripe avocado, halved, pitted, peeled, and chopped
- 1 cup shredded romaine lettuce
- 2 scallions, white and green parts, trimmed and chopped
  Cilantro, for garnish
  Tortilla chips, for serving

In a bowl, combine beans, lime juice, and water; season with salt and pepper. Transfer to a serving dish. Top with individual layers of sour cream, cheese, chiles, tomatoes, avocado, lettuce, and scallions. Garnish with cilantro. Serve with chips.

REFRIED BEANS

- 2 tablespoons olive oil
- 2 small onions, very finely chopped
- 1 dried bay leaf
  Coarse salt and freshly ground pepper
- 2 garlic cloves, minced
- 1 teaspoon chili powder
- 3 cans (15.5 ounces each) pinto beans, rinsed and drained
- ⅔ cup water, plus more as needed

1. In a saucepan, heat oil over medium-high. Add onions and bay leaf; season with salt and pepper. Cook, stirring, until onions are translucent, about 6 minutes. Add garlic and chili powder; cook, stirring, until garlic is softened and mixture is fragrant, about 3 minutes. Discard bay leaf.

2. Add two-thirds of the pinto beans and stir to coat. Add the water and mash mixture using a potato masher. Add remaining pinto beans and stir to combine; add more water, if necessary, to thin. Season with salt and pepper, and keep warm until ready to use.

Watercress Salad with Pepitas

Get in the habit of putting a green salad on the table for even the most casual gathering, but keep it simple: No salad should have more ingredients than you can count on your fingers.

- 3 tablespoons plus 1 teaspoon olive oil
- ⅓ cup pepitas
- 2 tablespoons white-wine vinegar
- ½ teaspoon ground cumin
  Coarse salt and freshly ground pepper
- 1½ pounds watercress, tough stems removed

1. Heat 1 teaspoon oil in a heavy cast-iron skillet over medium. Add pepitas and cook until puffed and golden, about 4 minutes. (Store at room temperature up to 1 day.)

2. In a large bowl, combine vinegar and cumin; whisk in remaining 3 tablespoons oil. Season with salt and pepper. (To store, cover and refrigerate up to 2 days.) Add watercress and toss to combine. Serve topped with pepitas.

Hearty Beef Chili

Having a good chili recipe in your back pocket will serve you well for years to come. (Better yet, have two: a beef chili and, for vegetarian friends, something meatless, like the recipe that follows.) The stew is simple to throw together and keeps well. You'll need to heat it up just before everyone arrives. Then set out all the toppings (arguably the best part).

8	whole dried chiles (5 ancho and 3 guajillo or all ancho; about 3 ounces)
	Hot water
3	tablespoons safflower oil, plus more as needed
3	pounds trimmed beef chuck, cut into $\frac{1}{2}$-inch pieces
	Coarse salt and freshly ground pepper
2	large onions, coarsely chopped
7 or 8	garlic cloves, minced (5 tablespoons)
2	jalapeño or serrano chiles (ribs and seeds removed for less heat, if desired), minced
$2\frac{1}{2}$	teaspoons ground cumin
$1\frac{1}{2}$	teaspoons dried oregano
1	can (28 ounces) whole peeled plum tomatoes, pureed with their juices
4	cups water, plus more for soaking and as needed
2 to 3	teaspoons distilled white vinegar, to taste
	Sour cream, tortilla strips, cilantro, and grated cheese, for serving

1. Toast dried chiles in a dry skillet over medium-high heat until fragrant and blistered, 2 to 3 minutes per side. Remove stems and seeds; discard. Transfer chiles to a large measuring cup or bowl, and cover with hot water. Place a small bowl on top to keep chiles submerged and let soak for 30 minutes. Remove chiles from water and puree in a blender with $\frac{1}{2}$ cup of the soaking liquid.

2. Heat a large, heavy pot over high. Add 2 tablespoons oil. Season beef with $2\frac{1}{2}$ teaspoons salt and $\frac{1}{2}$ teaspoon pepper. Brown beef in batches, adding more oil as needed, about 10 minutes. Transfer to a plate. Add remaining tablespoon oil, the onions, garlic, and minced chiles to pot, and cook over medium-high heat until onions are translucent, about 5 minutes. (If the pan gets too dark, add a little water and scrape up browned bits with a wooden spoon to deglaze.) Add cumin and oregano, and cook, stirring constantly, until fragrant, 30 seconds to 1 minute.

3. Stir in browned beef and chile puree. Add tomato puree, the water, and $\frac{1}{2}$ teaspoon salt. Bring to a boil. Reduce heat and simmer gently, partially covered, until meat is very tender and juices are thick, $2\frac{1}{2}$ to 3 hours. (Check pot once an hour; if chili seems dry, add a little water.) Season chili with salt and stir in vinegar. Serve with toppings. (Chili can be refrigerated for up to 3 days; reheat in a pot over medium, stirring occasionally.)

Vegetarian Green Chili

Tomatillos—the small yellowish fruits enveloped in papery husks—give this chili a refreshing tartness. Adjust the spiciness by choosing hot or mild canned green chiles.

3	pounds tomatillos, husked and washed
2	tablespoons extra-virgin olive oil
1	large onion, chopped
1	poblano chile, ribs and seeds removed for less heat, chopped
4	garlic cloves, minced
	Coarse salt
1	can (4 ounces) diced green chiles
1	tablespoon plus $1\frac{1}{2}$ teaspoons chili powder
2	teaspoons ground cumin
6	cups cooked beans, such as white or kidney beans, rinsed and drained
2	cups water
	Sour cream, tortilla strips, cilantro, lime wedges, and grated cheese, for serving

1. In a food processor or blender, puree tomatillos until smooth. In a large Dutch oven or other heavy pot, heat oil over medium-high. Add onion, poblano, and garlic; season with salt. Cook, stirring occasionally, until onion is translucent, about 4 minutes. Stir in green chiles, chili powder, and cumin; cook, stirring frequently, until spices are darkened and fragrant, about 3 minutes.

2. Add beans, tomatillos, and the water; bring to a boil over high heat. Reduce to a simmer, and cook until beans are tender and chili is thickened, 20 to 30 minutes. Serve with toppings.

PREP PLAN

Two Days Before

Prepare beef chili

Make dressing
for salad

One Day Before

Prepare
vegetarian chili

Toast pepitas
for the salad

Toast pecans
for the cake

The Day Of

Bake the cake and
cool completely

Prep ingredients
for the dip

Bake the
cornbread

**Just Before
Guests Arrive**

Top cake with
icing and pecans

Prepare refried
beans; assemble
the dip

Reheat both chilis

Toss the salad
with the dressing

Skillet Cornbread

Vegetable oil, for pan

1 cup fine yellow cornmeal, preferably stone-ground

¼ cup all-purpose flour

⅓ cup sugar

1 teaspoon baking powder

½ teaspoon baking soda

½ teaspoon coarse salt

1 cup buttermilk

½ cup milk

1 large egg, lightly beaten

2 tablespoons unsalted butter, melted and cooled

1. Preheat oven to 425°F. Lightly oil an 8-inch cast-iron skillet and heat in oven. Meanwhile, whisk together cornmeal, flour, sugar, baking powder, baking soda, and salt in a large bowl. Combine buttermilk, milk, and egg in another bowl. Add buttermilk mixture to cornmeal mixture and whisk to combine. Add melted butter, whisking to incorporate.

2. Remove skillet from oven and pour in batter (it will sizzle). Bake until dark golden around the edges and set in center, 25 to 30 minutes. Let cool slightly in pan before cutting into squares or wedges. Serve warm or at room temperature.

Texas Sheet Cake

This bake–sale and potluck staple is moist, dense, and ultra–chocolaty. We lined the pan with parchment to make it easier to transfer the cake to a serving platter.

For cake

1 cup (2 sticks) unsalted butter, plus more (room temperature) for pan

2 cups all-purpose flour

2 cups granulated sugar

1 teaspoon baking soda

1 teaspoon coarse salt

½ teaspoon ground cinnamon

¼ cup unsweetened natural cocoa powder

1 cup water

2 large eggs, lightly beaten

½ cup buttermilk

1 teaspoon pure vanilla extract

For icing

6 tablespoons unsalted butter

3 tablespoons unsweetened natural cocoa powder

6 tablespoons heavy cream

1½ teaspoons pure vanilla extract

1¾ cups plus 2 tablespoons confectioners' sugar, sifted

1 cup chopped toasted pecans

1. Make the cake: Preheat oven to 375°F. Butter a 9-by-13-inch baking pan. Line with parchment, leaving a 2-inch overhang on long sides. In a large heatproof bowl, whisk together flour, granulated sugar, baking soda, salt, and cinnamon.

2. Melt butter in a saucepan over medium-low heat. Whisk in cocoa, then the water. Raise heat to medium-high and bring to a boil, whisking occasionally. Pour over flour mixture; stir to combine. Stir in eggs, buttermilk, and vanilla. Pour batter into prepared pan; smooth top with an offset spatula. Bake until a tester inserted in center comes out clean, 22 to 24 minutes.

3. Make the icing: In a small saucepan, bring butter, cocoa, and cream to a boil, stirring occasionally. Remove from heat; whisk in vanilla and confectioners' sugar. Let stand until warm before using. Transfer cake in pan to a wire rack; let cool 15 minutes. Pour glaze over cake. Sprinkle with pecans and let cool before serving.

FONDUE DINNER

Invite a few close friends for an evening of warm wintry Alpine comforts—après-ski, après-skate, or après-nothing-too-strenuous-at-all. There's no heavy lifting involved in composing this cozy, help-yourself supper. **SERVES 6**

The Menu Smoked Trout and Celery Root Salad with Rye Crisps ■ Bitter Greens Salad ■ Cheese Fondue with Seared Steak and Vegetables ■ Lemon Ginger Cookies ■ Roasted Brandied Pears ■ Coffee with Cardamom and Cognac

Smoked Trout and Celery Root Salad with Rye Crisps

Think of this as more of an assembly idea than a recipe. Buy some nice smoked trout, mash some briny capers into creamy butter, and toss celery root with a splash of vinegar and little else. Let guests top their own crackers as one of you pours the wine and the other prepares the fondue.

½ cup (1 stick) unsalted butter, room temperature

2 tablespoons capers, rinsed and drained

1 small celery root, peeled, thinly sliced, and cut into matchsticks

2 tablespoons distilled white vinegar

Coarse salt and freshly ground pepper

¼ cup finely chopped fresh dill

1 (8-ounce) package smoked trout

Rye crisp crackers, such as Finn Crisp

Mix butter and capers in a small bowl until well combined. In a separate bowl, toss celery root with vinegar. Season with salt and pepper, and top with dill. Serve trout with crackers, caper butter, and celery root salad.

Bitter Greens Salad

Bitter greens come in many colors and textures—silky pale endive, spiky frisée, and radicchio that's speckled (*Variegato di Castelfranco*) or saturated red (*di Treviso* and *di Gorizia*), among others. Their bitterness varies in intensity as well. Mix and match milder and more bitter greens for a sensational salad balanced by a gently sweet vinaigrette.

1 tablespoon plus 1 teaspoon white-wine vinegar

3 tablespoons extra-virgin olive oil

½ teaspoon sugar

Coarse salt and freshly ground pepper

2 heads endive, cored and thinly sliced crosswise

1 head frisée, cored and torn into bite-size pieces

1 head radicchio, cored and thinly sliced

In a large bowl, whisk together vinegar, oil, and sugar. Season with salt and pepper. Add greens and toss just before serving.

PREP PLAN

Up to One Week Before

Bake cookies

Make syrup for coffee

One Day Before

Blanch potatoes, broccoli, and cauliflower, and prep the other vegetables (fennel and radishes) for fondue

Make caper butter for appetizer

The Day Of

Cut steak, grate cheeses, core and slice apple, and cube bread for fondue

Prep greens for salad

Cut celery root into matchsticks for appetizer

Just Before Guests Arrive

Toss together salad

Caramelize the pears for dessert

Reheat syrup for coffee

FONDUE 101

Fondue may be casual, but there are still a few things to keep in mind when you're the hosts:

Sharing Four to six is an ideal number of people dipping into the same fondue. Give each guest a coded fondue fork to avoid mix-ups when the forks are in the pot. Resist the urge to double the recipe—it's better to make multiple batches and replace as needed.

Prepping Blanch and cut up vegetables a day ahead; store with damp paper towels in resealable plastic bags until ready to use. Slice and cube bread in advance and allow pieces to dry out so that the cheese will adhere better. Choose the right types of cheeses, too: not all melt well.

Melting The impulse is often to turn the heat up to high in hopes of melting the cheese quickly. But this can cause the cheese to break (separating into a solid and a liquid) or "seize," its proteins clumping into a rubbery mass. Instead, add the cheese gradually and allow the fondue to cook slowly.

Dipping Use a fondue fork to spear a piece of bread, cooked steak, vegetable, or fruit. Hold the coated piece briefly over the pot to let drips fall back into the pot. Remove the food from the fondue fork onto a plate and eat with a dinner fork.

Cheese Fondue with Seared Steak and Vegetables

By its nature, cheese fondue is drippy and gooey and warm, so it instantly sets a relaxed and easy dinnertime mood. Typically, a blend of Swiss mountain cheeses (including Gruyère) is used, but adding young Gouda to the mix makes it tangier, milkier, and lighter in flavor. The combination makes a delicious dip for seared sirloin, boiled vegetables, cubes of bread, apple wedges, sliced fennel, and cornichons.

1	pound sirloin steak, cut into $1\frac{1}{2}$-inch pieces
	Coarse salt and freshly ground pepper
1	tablespoon safflower or other vegetable oil
1	pound small potatoes, such as red, new, or German Butterball
1	small head broccoli
1	small head cauliflower
8	ounces young Gouda, rind trimmed, coarsely grated
8	ounces Gruyère, rind trimmed, coarsely grated
2	tablespoons cornstarch
1	garlic clove, halved
$1\frac{1}{2}$	cups dry white wine
1	tablespoon brandy
	Freshly grated nutmeg
1	small bulb fennel, cored and cut into wedges
8	radishes, thinly sliced
1	apple, cored and sliced
$\frac{1}{2}$	cup cornichons
$\frac{1}{2}$	loaf rustic bread, cut into 1-inch cubes

1. Season beef with salt and pepper. Heat a heavy skillet over medium-high. Swirl in oil. Working in batches, add beef in a single layer. Cook, turning occasionally, until browned on all sides, about 3 minutes for medium-rare. Transfer to a plate; tent with parchment-lined foil.

2. Place potatoes and 1 teaspoon salt in a large saucepan with enough cold water to cover. Bring to a boil over high heat. Reduce to a simmer and cook until the tip of a paring knife inserted into center of potatoes meets only slight resistance, 15 to 20 minutes. Drain and reserve.

3. Meanwhile, bring another pot of water to a boil. Cut broccoli and cauliflower into 2- to 3-inch pieces. Add salt to water, then blanch broccoli and cauliflower florets until just tender, 5 minutes. Drain and reserve.

4. Toss cheeses with cornstarch in a bowl until coated. Rub bottom and sides of a fondue pot or medium pot with garlic; discard garlic. Add wine and brandy; bring to a simmer over medium-high heat.

5. Reduce heat to medium. Stir in cheese mixture in batches, waiting for cheeses to melt before adding more. Cook, stirring, until melted and smooth, about 10 minutes. Season with nutmeg.

6. Transfer mixture to a fondue pot set over a warmer. Serve immediately with beef, vegetables, apple, cornichons, and bread.

Lemon Ginger Cookies

To make things more visually interesting, and to carry on with the help-yourself feel of the evening, keep the dessert course loose and carefree: Set out the roasted pears, then place some drop cookies on a platter, with squares of store-bought dark chocolate, dried fruits, and toasted nuts.

½ cup (1 stick) unsalted butter, room temperature

¾ cup plus 2 tablespoons sugar, plus more for sprinkling

1 large egg

1 tablespoon finely grated lemon zest (from 1 lemon)

1⅓ cups all-purpose flour

½ teaspoon ground ginger

½ teaspoon baking soda

¼ teaspoon salt

1 tablespoon diced crystallized ginger, plus 3 tablespoons slivered

1. Preheat oven to 350°F. Line two baking sheets with parchment. With an electric mixer, cream butter and sugar on medium-high until light and fluffy, about 5 minutes, scraping down sides of bowl. Add egg; mix on high to combine. Add zest; mix to combine.

2. In a bowl, whisk together flour, ground ginger, baking soda, salt, and diced crystallized ginger; add to butter mixture and mix on medium-low just to combine.

3. Using two spoons, drop about 2 teaspoons of batter 3 inches apart on baking sheets. Bake cookies 7 minutes. Sprinkle cookies with sugar, top each with a few ginger slivers, rotate sheets, and bake until cookies are just golden, about 7 minutes more. Slide parchment with cookies onto a wire rack and let cool, about 15 minutes. (Store in airtight containers up to 1 week.)

Roasted Brandied Pears

Most people think of strawberries and peaches when they think of fresh fruit desserts, but pears are fantastic throughout the fall and winter, and just as worthy of a party menu. Roasting them in a little butter, sugar, and brandy is a good way to do just that. An ovenproof skillet lets you go from stovetop to roasting to tabletop with just one pan, but you can transfer the fruit to a serving dish if you like.

2 tablespoons unsalted butter

½ cup sugar

3 ripe but firm pears, such as Anjou or Bosc, halved

2 tablespoons brandy

Preheat oven to 350°F. Melt butter in an ovenproof skillet, preferably cast iron, over medium heat. Sprinkle sugar over melted butter, and cook, without stirring, until sugar caramelizes, about 5 minutes. Add pears, cut-side down, in an even layer. Carefully add brandy to deglaze pan. Spoon some caramelized sugar over pears, transfer skillet to oven, and roast until pears are lightly browned, about 20 minutes. Serve with pan juices.

Coffee with Cardamom and Cognac

You can always just make a pot of coffee, but why not end the meal with something out of the ordinary? This coffee-and-nightcap-in-one offers a nice way to relax after the rich fondue. Whipped cream is entirely optional; offer milk on the side, too.

1 cup water

1 cup raw sugar, such as turbinado or Demerara

9 cardamom pods, lightly crushed

2 cups heavy cream

1 cup cognac or other brandy

3 cups freshly brewed coffee

1. In a saucepan, bring the water, sugar, and cardamom to a simmer over medium heat, stirring to dissolve sugar. (Syrup mixture can be refrigerated in an airtight container up to 1 week. Before using, gently reheat.)

2. When ready to serve, whip cream to soft peaks. Add brandy and hot coffee to saucepan with syrup mixture, and stir to combine. Divide among 6 glasses. Serve immediately, with whipped cream on the side.

BÁNH MÌ
BUFFET

For those evenings when you round up a few friends for some screen time (an awards show, maybe, or just a collective hang while you catch up on your favorite series), we offer this way–better–than–take-out binge. It's filled with dishes that work well at room temperature and that can (mostly) be enjoyed out of hand. **SERVES 8**

195
GATHER ROUND

The Menu Lychee Martinis ■ Mango Salad ■ Kale and Asian
Pear Salad ■ Summer Rolls ■ Bánh Mì ■ Carrot and Beet Salad ■
Coconut Rice Pudding ■ Vietnamese Iced Coffee

Lychee Martinis

Kick things off with a twist on vodka martinis, here
sweetened with lychee fruit. The fruit—which, underneath
its nubby red skin, is translucent and juicy, like a grape—
is available canned year-round, or fresh from Asian grocers
during the summer.

- 3 ounces vodka
- 1 ounce dry vermouth
- ⅓ cup lychee juice, reserved from can

  Lychee fruit, for garnish

Fill a cocktail shaker halfway with ice. Add vodka,
vermouth, and lychee juice. Shake well. Strain into 2 martini
glasses and garnish each with a lychee.

Mango Salad

This refreshing salad serves as a delicious side dish for the
summer rolls, but if you put everything out all at once, you
may find that some of it makes its way into the rolls, too.

- 2 very firm underripe mangoes (about 2 pounds)
- ⅓ cup Nuoc Cham Dipping Sauce (page 199)
- 6 scallions, white and pale-green parts only
  (reserve dark green tops for Summer Rolls, page 199),
  thinly sliced on the diagonal
- ¼ cup lightly packed fresh mint leaves, coarsely chopped
- ½ cup lightly packed fresh cilantro leaves
  and stems, coarsely chopped
- ⅔ cup roasted unsalted peanuts, coarsely chopped

Peel mangoes. Cut ¼-inch-thick slices of flesh away from pits,
then cut slices lengthwise into ¼-inch-thick batons. In a large
bowl, gently toss together mangoes, dipping sauce, scallions, and
herbs. Let salad stand, stirring occasionally, 30 minutes. Before
serving, stir in peanuts. (Salad can be made 1 day ahead and stored
in refrigerator; bring to room temperature before serving.)

Kale and Asian Pear Salad

This is one of those recipes you'll find yourself trying once
and then finding excuses to make again. It's fantastic with
grilled chicken and steak.

- ¼ cup unseasoned rice vinegar
- 2 teaspoons soy sauce, or more to taste
- ½ teaspoon Dijon mustard
- 1 small garlic clove, minced
- 1 teaspoon grated peeled fresh ginger

  Pinch of red-pepper flakes
- ⅓ cup vegetable oil, such as safflower
- 1 bunch curly kale, tough stems and ribs
  removed, leaves torn
- 1 Asian pear, cored, quartered, and thinly sliced
- 1 small bunch flowering Asian greens, such as tatsoi

In a small bowl, whisk together vinegar, soy sauce, mustard, garlic,
ginger, and red-pepper flakes. Add oil in a slow, steady stream
until emulsified. (Dressing can be refrigerated in an airtight
container for up to 1 week.) Reserve half the dressing for Carrot
and Beet Salad (page 200). In a large bowl, combine kale,
pear, and Asian greens; toss with remaining dressing and serve.

Summer Rolls

You can make shrimp and vegetarian rolls in advance, or set things out and invite everyone to roll their own. The prep work is all done ahead of time, so all you have to do is lay out the building blocks (fresh herbs, crisp vegetables, shrimp, salty–sweet dipping sauces) and let guests go to town.

- 1 pound large shrimp (about 16 to 20), in shells
- 12 ounces rice vermicelli (rice stick noodles)
- 1 small head napa cabbage, halved, cored, and thinly sliced
- 7 medium carrots, sliced into ribbons with a spiral cutter (alternatively, cut into 1/8-by-3-inch matchsticks)
- 2 English cucumber or 8 Persian cucumbers, cut into 1/2-by-5 inch wedges
- 2 ripe avocados, halved, pitted, and thinly sliced
- 6 scallions, dark-green tops only (reserve white and pale-green parts for Mango Salad, page 196)
- 1 bunch fresh Thai or Italian basil
- 1 bunch fresh mint
- 1 bunch fresh cilantro
- 1 package (12 ounces) 8-inch rice-paper wrappers

  Nuoc Cham and Peanut Dipping Sauces (recipes follow), for serving

  Sambal oelek (Indonesian chili paste) or spicy chili sauce, for serving

1. Bring 1 inch water to a boil in a large, deep, straight-sided skillet. Submerge shrimp; immediately remove from heat and cover. Let stand 3 minutes; drain. Let shrimp cool, then peel. Cut in half lengthwise and devein. (Shrimp can be refrigerated in an airtight container up to 1 day.)

2. In a large bowl, pour boiling water over vermicelli and soak 15 minutes; drain and rinse. (Vermicelli can be refrigeratored in an airtight container up to 1 day.) Divide into equal portions.

3. Submerge cabbage and carrots in 2 separate bowls of ice water for 30 minutes; drain. Place alongside cucumber, avocados, scallions, basil, mint, cilantro, shrimp, and noodles on a platter.

4. Pour at least 1 inch warm water into a bowl slightly larger than rice-paper wrappers. Submerge 1 wrapper in warm water until pliable but still firm, about 10 seconds. (Replace warm water as necessary.) Transfer to a plate.

5. Place a layer of fillings on bottom third of each wrapper, leaving a 1½-inch border. Top with a portion of noodles and another layer of fillings. Fold bottom of wrapper tightly over fillings.

6. Roll once, tuck in sides, and finish rolling. Transfer roll to a plate and cover with a slightly damp paper towel; repeat steps 4 through 6 for remaining rolls. Serve with dipping sauces, or refrigerate for up to 2 hours.

NUOC CHAM DIPPING SAUCE

- 4 teaspoons minced garlic
- 2 Thai chiles or 1 serrano chile, stems and seeds removed, minced
- 2 tablespoons sugar
- 2 tablespoons hot water
- 1/2 cup fish sauce, such as nam pla or nuoc mam
- 1/2 cup unseasoned rice vinegar
- 4 teaspoons finely grated lime zest plus 3 tablespoons juice (from 2 limes)

Combine garlic, chiles, and sugar in a bowl. Add hot water, stirring until sugar has dissolved. Stir in fish sauce and vinegar, then lime zest and juice until combined. (Sauce can be refrigerated up to 1 day.)

PEANUT DIPPING SAUCE

- 1 teaspoon safflower oil
- 1 tablespoon minced garlic
- 2 tablespoons tomato paste
- 2 tablespoons hoisin sauce
- 1/2 cup creamy peanut butter
- 1¼ cups water

  Roasted unsalted peanuts, coarsely chopped, for garnish

1. Heat oil in a small saucepan over medium-high. Add garlic, tomato paste, and hoisin, and cook, stirring occasionally, until mixture comes to a boil, about 1 minute. Add 1/4 cup peanut butter and 1 cup water and return to a boil, whisking until mixture is smooth and thoroughly incorporated.

2. Reduce heat to medium-low and simmer until thickened and slightly darkened, about 3 minutes. Remove from heat; whisk in remaining 1/4 cup each peanut butter and water, and let cool. Divide among dipping bowls and garnish with peanuts.

Bánh Mì

One piece of roasted pork, sliced for bánh mì sandwiches, is a delicious, economical, and efficient way to feed a crowd. As with the Summer Rolls (page 199), you can make up just a few: Guests can embellish their sandwiches with some of the same vegetables offered for the summer rolls. Here sweet potatoes are cut into rounds, so they cook more quickly and so they are easy to mash into the bread for meatless sandwiches. Be sure the cut pieces are similar sizes, for even cooking.

For marinade

1	small shallot, finely chopped
1/3	cup packed light-brown sugar
1/4	cup fish sauce, such as nam pla or nuoc mam
2	tablespoons unseasoned rice vinegar
1	teaspoon freshly ground pepper
2	garlic cloves, thinly sliced
2	teaspoons safflower oil
2	teaspoons coarse salt

For sandwiches

1½	pounds pork tenderloin
3	medium sweet potatoes, scrubbed and cut crosswise into 1-inch rounds
	Coarse salt
1	tablespoon olive oil
	Nuoc Cham Dipping Sauce (page 199)
2	baguettes, cut into quarters and lightly toasted
	Mint and cilantro sprigs, for serving

For Sriracha mayo

1/2	cup mayonnaise
2	tablespoons Sriracha

1. Make marinade: Whisk together all marinade ingredients; set aside 1/4 cup for sweet potatoes. Set pork in a shallow dish and pour remaining marinade over pork; refrigerate for at least 20 minutes and up to overnight.

2. Preheat oven to 400°F. On a large rimmed baking sheet, toss sweet potatoes with the reserved 1/4 cup marinade; season with salt. Spread into a single layer; roast, flipping slices halfway through, until tender and lightly browned, about 25 minutes.

3. Meanwhile, heat oil in a large ovenproof skillet over medium-high. Remove pork from marinade, allowing excess to drip off. Add to skillet, and cook, browning on all sides, about 5 minutes. Transfer skillet to oven and roast pork, uncovered, until a meat thermometer inserted into the center of tenderloin registers 145°F, about 12 minutes. Remove and let rest 5 minutes, then thinly slice pork against the grain.

4. To make Sriracha mayonnaise: In a small serving bowl, mix mayonnaise and Sriracha. Serve pork and sweet potatoes with Sriracha mayonnaise, Nuoc Cham Dipping Sauce, bread, mint, and cilantro.

Carrot and Beet Salad

4	large carrots (mix of yellow and orange)
2	medium beets, peeled
2	tablespoons unseasoned rice vinegar
2	tablespoons mirin
1/4	teaspoon salt
	Pinch of freshly ground pepper

Using a spiral cutter, slice carrots and beets into long, thin ribbons and place them in a bowl. (Alternatively, cut vegetables into matchsticks or coarsely shred with the large holes on a box grater.) In a small bowl, whisk together vinegar, mirin, salt, and pepper. Pour vinaigrette over vegetables, toss, and serve.

Coconut Rice Pudding

Creamy rice pudding gets even creamier with short-grained Arborio rice, which stays beautifully firm when cooked—because nobody likes a mushy rice pudding.

1	cup Arborio or sushi rice, rinsed and drained
5¼	cups milk
2¼	cups canned unsweetened coconut milk, well stirred
1½	teaspoons pure vanilla extract
½	cup sugar
½	teaspoon coarse salt
½	cup unsweetened coconut flakes, toasted
2	small star fruit, cut crosswise into ¼-inch slices

In a large saucepan, bring rice, both milks, vanilla, sugar, and salt to a boil. Reduce heat to medium and simmer, stirring frequently, until rice is tender and most liquid is absorbed, 25 to 30 minutes. Rice pudding can be served warm, room temperature, or cold (refrigerate at least 1 hour and up to 3 days). Before serving, top with toasted coconut flakes and star fruit and, if desired, additional whisked coconut milk.

Vietnamese Iced Coffee

Try this instead of coffee ice cream at the end of your meal; it's a strong brew that drips through a special metal filter, called a *phin*, into a glass with sweetened condensed milk in the bottom. It's utterly delicious and habit-forming.

1 to 2	tablespoons sweetened condensed milk, to taste
1	heaping tablespoon ground Vietnamese coffee, such as Trung Nguyen

1. Pour sweetened condensed milk into a tall, narrow heatproof glass.

2. Remove lid and insert from filter. Place ground coffee in base of filter; tap to settle into an even layer. Place insert on top of coffee; adjust to even out grounds and secure in place (do not pack). Place filter on top of glass.

3. Wet coffee with simmering water (it should rise just above insert); wait for grounds to absorb water, about 20 seconds. Add more simmering water, filling to top of filter chamber. Top with lid. Let drip through, 4 to 5 minutes. Remove filter. Fill glass with ice. Serve with a spoon (to stir) and a straw.

PREP PLAN

Up to One Week Before

Prepare dressing
for kale salad

Two to Three Days Before

Make peanut sauce
for summer rolls

Prepare coconut rice pudding

One Day Before

Cook vermicelli and
boil shrimp for summer rolls

Prepare nuoc cham sauce for
summer rolls and bánh mì

Prepare mango salad

Marinate pork for bánh mì

Make Sriracha mayonnaise
for bánh mì

The Day Of

Prep produce (except avocado);
wrap in damp paper towels and
refrigerate

Prepare summer rolls
(up to 2 hours ahead) and
bring both dipping sauces to
room temperature

Roast sweet potatoes and toast
baguettes for bánh mì

Bring mango salad to room
temperature

Just Before Guests Arrive

Prepare cocktail

Cook pork for bánh mì
and set out all the ingredients
for assembly

WEEKEND BRUNCH

The two-meals-in-one situation known as brunch lends itself beautifully to setting out a buffet of room-temperature foods and then actually sitting down yourself for the next few hours. Host one and you may quickly discover that it's your new favorite way to invite people over, hands down. **SERVES 8**

The Menu Rosé Grapefruit Cocktails ▪ Melon with Mint ▪ Rhubarb Compote with Greek Yogurt ▪ Seared Ham Steak ▪ Roasted Asparagus ▪ Soft-Boiled Eggs with Seasoned Salt ▪ Streusel Coffee Cake

Rosé Grapefruit Cocktails

For brunch, consider making a few pitchers of this citrusy cocktail just before everyone arrives and replenishing as needed. Look for Lillet Rose or Blanc, an aperitif wine from France, at your local wine shop.

1	cup Lillet Rose or Blanc, chilled
½	cup fresh pink or Ruby Red grapefruit juice, chilled

Divide wine and juice among 4 glasses. Fill glasses with ice and stir.

Melon with Mint

1	ripe melon, such as honeydew or cantaloupe
	Small mint sprigs
	Lime wedges

Slice melon into wedges and remove peel. In a serving bowl, combine melon and mint sprigs. Squeeze lime wedges over top and gently toss.

Rhubarb Compote with Greek Yogurt

When tangy yogurt meets bold rhubarb in a compote mellowed with sugar and a vanilla bean, it's an ideal partnership.

1¾	pounds rhubarb, ends trimmed, cut crosswise into 1½-inch pieces (about 6 cups)
1	cup sugar
1	vanilla bean, split lengthwise and seeds scraped
32	ounces Greek yogurt

1. Stir rhubarb and sugar together in a large saucepan off heat; let stand until rhubarb releases some liquid, about 10 minutes.

2. Bring rhubarb mixture and vanilla bean and seeds to a boil over medium-high heat, stirring occasionally. Reduce heat; simmer, stirring occasionally, until rhubarb is starting to break down but some whole pieces remain, about 5 minutes. Remove from heat. (Compote can be refrigerated up to 2 days.)

3. Let compote cool completely before serving with yogurt.

PREP PLAN

Five Days Before

Prepare seasoned salt for eggs

Two Days Before

Bake coffee cake

Make rhubarb compote

One Day Before

Juice grapefruit and chill

Chill Lillet

The Day Of

Slice melon, and cut limes into wedges

Roast asparagus

Just Before Guests Arrive

Prepare grapefruit cocktails

Sear ham steaks

Soft-boil eggs

Toss melon with mint

ASPARAGUS 101

Choosing

Pick smooth, unwrinkled stalks with tightly closed tips and no flowering. Thickness is a matter of taste: Thicker, meatier stalks are usually sweeter but just as tender as the thin ones. Avoid stalks that are flattened, wrinkled, or that feel hollow.

Storing

Keep asparagus in a plastic bag in the crisper drawer away from ethylene–producing fruit like apples and pears, which toughen the stalks. Note that storing bunches upright in water may cause the tips to open.

Rinsing and Trimming

The tender tips can be sandy; holding the bunch upside down, gently swish them in cold water. To trim, snap off the tough woody bottoms: Bend the stalk at the natural breaking point (you can usually find it by softly bending or looking for a shift in color), 1 to 2 inches from the base.

Seared Ham Steak

Bacon? Been there. Sausage? Done that. Sear a ham steak and you get all the meaty satisfaction without the fuss.

| 2 to 2½ | pounds fully-cooked bone-in ham steaks |
| 2 | tablespoons pure maple syrup |

Lightly brush both sides of ham steaks with maple syrup. Working in two batches, sear ham in a large skillet over medium-high heat until golden brown and caramelized on both sides, about 2 to 3 minutes per side.

Roasted Asparagus

Roasting whole asparagus spears yields heartier flavor and a softer texture than blanching or steaming them.

1½	pounds medium-thick asparagus
2	teaspoons olive oil
⅛	teaspoon coarse salt
	Pinch of freshly ground pepper

Preheat oven to 475°F. Trim asparagus, then toss with oil, salt, and pepper on a rimmed baking sheet. Spread in a single layer. Roast until tender, 10 to 15 minutes, depending on thickness.

Soft-Boiled Eggs with Seasoned Salt

Despite its name, eggs shouldn't really be boiled all the way through the cooking process—a method that can yield a rubbery result. Instead, bring eggs just to a boil and then immediately remove them from the heat.

1	dozen large eggs
2	teaspoons coarse salt
2	teaspoons black sesame seeds
1	teaspoon dried fennel seeds
1	teaspoon ground ginger

1. Place eggs in a saucepan large enough to accommodate a single layer. Fill pan with cold water, covering eggs by an inch. Bring to a boil over medium-high heat. Immediately take off heat, cover, and let stand 6 minutes. Remove eggs from water and serve.

2. Combine salt, sesame seeds, fennel seeds, and ground ginger in a small bowl until well blended. Serve with eggs. (Salt can be kept in an airtight container at room temperature up to 1 month.)

Streusel Coffee Cake

Anyone who is interested in hosting people for breakfast would be well advised to commit a good coffee-cake recipe to memory, and this may be just the one. It mixes up quickly and easily, and conjures childhood memories, aromas, and flavors with each bite. Streusel, derived from an Old German word that means "something strewn," adds a sweet crunch to this sour-cream cake. The glaze is entirely optional, but it definitely dresses up the cake for company.

For the streusel

- 1¾ cups all-purpose flour
- 1 cup packed light-brown sugar
- 1¼ teaspoons ground cinnamon
- Coarse salt
- ¾ cup (1½ sticks) cold unsalted butter, cut into small pieces
- 1½ cups coarsely chopped toasted pecans

For the cake

- ½ cup (1 stick) unsalted butter, room temperature, plus
- more for pan
- 2 cups all-purpose flour
- 1¼ teaspoons baking powder
- ½ teaspoon baking soda
- Coarse salt
- 1 cup granulated sugar
- 2 large eggs
- 1½ teaspoons pure vanilla extract
- 1 cup sour cream

For the glaze

- 1 cup confectioners' sugar
- 2 tablespoons milk

1. Make streusel. For topping: Whisk together flour, ¾ cup brown sugar, 1 teaspoon cinnamon, and 1 teaspoon salt. Cut in butter using a pastry cutter, or rub in with your fingers until small to medium clumps form. Mix in ½ cup pecans. (Refrigerate until ready to use.) For streusel center: Mix together remaining ¼ cup brown sugar, ¼ teaspoon cinnamon, and 1 cup pecans.

2. Make cake: Preheat oven to 350°F. Butter a 9-inch tube pan with a removable bottom. Whisk together flour, baking powder, baking soda, and ½ teaspoon salt in a bowl.

3. Beat butter and granulated sugar with a mixer on medium speed until pale and fluffy, about 2 minutes. Beat in eggs, 1 at a time, then vanilla. Beat in flour mixture in 3 additions, alternating with sour cream, beginning and ending with flour. Beat until well combined.

4. Spoon half the batter into pan. Sprinkle streusel-center mixture evenly over batter. Top with remaining batter, and spread evenly using an offset spatula. Sprinkle streusel-topping mixture evenly over batter.

5. Bake until cake is golden brown and a toothpick inserted into the center comes out clean, about 55 minutes. Transfer pan to a wire rack and let cool completely. Remove cake from pan and transfer to parchment.

6. Make glaze: Whisk together confectioners' sugar and milk. Drizzle over cooled cake, letting it drip down sides. Let set for 5 minutes before serving. (The cake can be kept, tightly wrapped, at room temperature for up to 5 days.)

COFFEEMAKERS

There's a world of ways to brew a cup of Joe. Here are some of the most popular methods:

Automatic Drip Coffeemaker
For all-around ease and the ability to make several cups at a time, the drip coffeemaker is the best bet when hosting a crowd. Choose glass or thermal carafes to keep coffee warm.

The Pour-Over
This no-fuss (and inexpensive) method relies on a ceramic mesh cone with a paper filter, and lets you make single cups or a whole carafe. The downside: It's a hands-on method; no set and forget, as with a drip coffeemaker. The hourglass-shaped Chemex, a heat-resistant glass carafe accented with a wood collar, is pure minimalist style.

French Press
As easy as the pour-over, and almost as inexpensive, the French press is a glass carafe and plunger with a built-in mesh filter. It'll produce a thicker, more full-bodied brew, because the grounds have been fully submerged in the water.

Moka Espresso Pot
Want to feel like an Italian? Spoon some espresso into the bottom of this aluminum or stainless steel maker along with water; screw the bottom to the top pot and put it right on the burner. You won't confuse this cup with an espresso made with an electric machine, but it does have a bit more kick.

TACO FIESTA

The best party menus allow for a wide range of dietary preferences. Tacos fit the bill: Simply set out corn tortillas (naturally gluten-free) and different fillings (for carnivores and vegetarians alike), then let everyone do their own thing. Throw in icy drinks, crunchy starters, and easy sides; finish with fruity ice pops in pastel shades. Fun for everyone indeed! SERVES 8

213
GATHER ROUND

The Menu New Classic Margaritas ▪ Three Amigos Cocktails ▪ Mexican Corn Salad ▪ Quick–Pickled Radishes and Onions ▪ Spicy Pineapple Slaw ▪ Smoky Salsa ▪ Ancho Chicken and Oregano Cod Tacos ▪ Butternut Squash and Rajas Tacos ▪ Jicama and Cucumber Spears with Citrus Vinaigrette ▪ Frozen Fruit Pops

New Classic Margaritas

The true margarita balances sour, sweet, and salty sensations against the electrifying flavor of Mexico's most famous spirit, tequila. Before serving, run a lime wedge over each glass and dip the rim in coarse salt.

- 6 ounces silver tequila (¾ cup)
- 3 ounces Cointreau (¼ cup plus 2 tablespoons)
- 2 teaspoons superfine sugar
- 2 tablespoons plus 2 teaspoons fresh lime juice, plus lime wedges, for garnish and for rims of glasses
- 1 tablespoon plus 1 teaspoon fresh lemon juice, plus lemon wedges, for garnish
- 1 tablespoon plus 1 teaspoon fresh orange juice, plus orange wedges, for garnish
- 4 cups small ice cubes

Combine all ingredients except citrus wedges in a pitcher. Divide citrus wedges among 4 glasses; pour margaritas over each.

Three Amigos Cocktails

Think of this as Mexico in a glass: the vivid flavor of fresh lime juice plus beer and salt. For a traditional finish, add a dash of hot sauce.

- 2 cups water
- 1¼ cups fresh lime juice (from 12 limes)
- ¼ cup superfine sugar
- 2 (12-ounce) bottles Mexican beer

Coarse salt, for serving

Hot sauce, for serving (optional)

Combine the water, lime juice, and sugar in a pitcher. Fill another pitcher with ice. Stir in beer and 1⅓ cups lime mixture, and pour into salt-rimmed glasses. Add a dash of hot sauce, if desired.

Mexican Corn Salad

This is a fresh take on elote (grilled Mexican street corn), but here the corn is served as a salad rather than on the cob.

- ¾ teaspoon sweet paprika
- ½ teaspoon light-brown sugar
- ¾ teaspoon chopped fresh thyme leaves

  Coarse salt
- 6 ears corn, shucked
- ½ jicama, peeled and cut in ½-inch pieces
- 2 small poblano chiles, seeded, stemmed, and cut in ½-inch pieces
- ½ cup fresh cilantro leaves
- 3 tablespoons extra-virgin olive oil
- 4½ ounces crumbled queso fresco (1 cup)
- 1 tablespoon fresh lime juice

1. In a bowl, combine paprika, sugar, thyme, and 1½ teaspoons salt.

2. Working in batches, char corn over flame of a gas stove, turning with tongs, until blackened, 3 to 4 minutes per cob. Transfer to a plate; let cool. Slice corn kernels from cobs into a large bowl.

3. Add jicama, poblanos, cilantro, oil, queso, lime juice, and 2 teaspoons paprika mixture. Lightly toss to mix.

Quick-Pickled Radishes and Onions

It requires less than an hour to take these vegetables from fresh to crisply pickled.

- 6 radishes, very thinly sliced
- ½ cup distilled white vinegar
- 1 large red onion, very thinly sliced

  Coarse salt

Toss radishes with ¼ cup vinegar in a bowl; toss onions with ¼ cup vinegar in another bowl. Season each with salt and let stand for at least 30 minutes and up to 3 days. Refrigerate until ready to serve.

Spicy Pineapple Slaw

This is fabulous served alongside tacos, but no one will mind if it's also layered into the tacos themselves. It's that kind of party.

- 5 cups finely shredded green cabbage (from 1 head)
- 3 carrots, very thinly sliced on the diagonal
- ½ red onion, very thinly sliced and rinsed in cold water
- 3 cups small chopped pineapple (from 1 pineapple)
- 2 jalapeños, ribs and seeds removed for less heat, if desired, minced
- ½ cup chopped fresh cilantro leaves
- ¼ cup chopped fresh mint leaves
- ¼ cup extra-virgin olive oil
- ⅓ cup fresh lime juice (from 4 limes)

  Coarse salt and freshly ground pepper

In a large bowl, combine cabbage, carrots, onion, pineapple, jalapeños, cilantro, and mint. Drizzle with oil and lime juice, and season with salt and pepper. Toss to combine. Let stand 30 minutes. Toss again before serving.

Smoky Salsa

If you're low on time or energy (or both), making your own salsa may be the first thing to take off your to-do list. But it's worth trying at least once—and taking note of just how incredible it tastes. As an added incentive, it's even better when made a day or two ahead. Here we used ripe red cocktail tomatoes. Larger than a cherry or grape tomato, the cocktail variety, despite its name, is not for martinis. But it does strike a lovely balance of sweetness and acidity, ideal for salsa.

- 1½ pounds cocktail tomatoes
- 1 small onion, cut into 8 pieces
- ½ teaspoon ancho chile powder
- 2 teaspoons adobo sauce from 1 can of chipotle chile peppers in adobo
- 1 tablespoon fresh lime juice
- ¼ teaspoon finely grated orange zest

  Coarse salt

Heat broiler with rack in top position. Place tomatoes and onion in a single layer on a rimmed baking sheet. Broil until vegetables are blistered, 10 to 15 minutes. Transfer to a food processor and pulse until coarsely pureed. Add chile powder, adobo sauce, lime juice, and orange zest; pulse to combine. Season with salt. (Salsa can be stored in an airtight container in the refrigerator for up to 5 days.)

PREP PLAN

Three Days Before

Prepare citrus vinaigrette

Pickle radishes and onions

Make frozen fruit pops

Two Days Before

Make salsa

One Day Before

Prepare limeade for cocktails

The Day Of

Toast pepitas

Juice citrus (for margaritas) and cut fruit into wedges

Slice cucumbers and jicama (up to 2 hours ahead)

Char corn for salad; let cool and shave off kernels

Prep ingredients for pineapple slaw

Prep garnishes for tacos

Just Before Guests Arrive

Toss together pineapple slaw

Bring salsa to room temperature

Coat rims of glasses with salt for margaritas

Prepare pitchers of cocktail and margaritas

Set out jicama and cucumbers with vinaigrette

Cook both taco fillings

Warm tortillas

CORN TORTILLAS

A warm corn tortilla, made simply from *masa harina* (corn flour) and water, is the foundation for almost every Mexican meal. It adds texture and flavor to whatever it holds—chicken, steak, pork, fish, beans, guacamole, you name it. Corn tortillas are generally made smaller and thicker than flour tortillas so they won't fall apart (they don't contain gluten, the stretchy protein in flour that helps hold the tortillas together); look for the standard 6-inch size.

You can make your own tortillas, of course. But you'll need a tortilla press to make them just the right thickness. Look for fresh tortillas at farmers' markets and Mexican groceries. High-quality packaged corn tortillas are inexpensive and practical for parties. And, if tightly sealed, they'll keep at room temperature for 5 days or in the refrigerator for 2 weeks.

Ancho Chicken and Oregano Cod Tacos

Offering a choice of chicken or fish (and the vegetarian option that follows) should keep everyone happy. For convenience and ease, we've combined chicken and cod fillings in one recipe, but each marinates and cooks separately. You could choose to make just one or the other, as long as the total weight is about the same.

1¾	pounds boneless, skinless chicken thighs (about 6 thighs)
2	pounds skinless cod or hake fillet
	Coarse salt
½	teaspoon ancho chile powder
1	teaspoon dried oregano, preferably Mexican
½	teaspoon finely grated orange zest, plus ⅓ cup fresh orange juice (from 2 oranges)
¼	teaspoon finely grated lime zest, plus 3 tablespoons fresh lime juice (from 2 limes)
3	tablespoons extra-virgin olive oil
2	garlic cloves, minced
24	corn tortillas, warmed
	Cilantro leaves, sliced avocado, lime wedges, sour cream, cotija cheese, toasted pepitas, and pickled jalapeños, for serving
	Smoky Salsa (page 217), for serving
	Quick-Pickled Radishes and Onions (page 217), for serving

1. Preheat oven to 450°F. Season chicken and fish with salt. Place each in a separate 9-by-13-inch baking dish, arranging fish skin-side down and chicken in a single layer. Sprinkle chicken with ancho and fish with oregano. In a small bowl, stir together orange juice and zest, lime juice and zest, oil, and garlic; divide citrus mixture between dishes.

2. Transfer dishes to oven. Bake until fish is cooked through, 12 to 16 minutes, basting once; remove fish from oven. Baste chicken once and continue to bake until cooked through, about 10 more minutes. Remove from oven and let cool slightly. Shred chicken with 2 forks; toss with cooking liquid. Place fish on a serving platter, spoon some cooking liquid over, and lightly flake with forks. Serve with tortillas, cilantro, avocado, lime, sour cream, cheese, toasted pepitas, pickled jalapeños, Smoky Salsa, and Quick-Pickled Radishes and Onions.

Butternut Squash and Rajas Tacos

Autumn squashes are wonderfully filling and flavorful in tacos and tostadas. Here we've paired hearty butternut with *rajas* (sautéed strips of poblano chiles and onions).

¼	cup extra-virgin olive oil
2	large poblano chiles, stems and seeds removed, thinly sliced
2	medium onions, thinly sliced
¼	medium butternut squash, peeled, seeded, and cut into 1-inch pieces
	Coarse salt and freshly ground pepper
½	teaspoon dried oregano, preferably Mexican
⅔	cup water, plus more as needed

1. Heat oil in a large straight-sided skillet over high. Add chiles and cook, stirring, 1 minute. Add onions and cook, stirring occasionally, until translucent, about 5 minutes. Stir in squash, and season with salt and pepper; cook, stirring, 1 minute. Stir in oregano.

2. Add the water. Cover, reduce heat to medium, and cook, stirring once or twice, until squash is tender and almost all liquid is absorbed, 6 to 8 minutes, adding more water if needed.

Jicama and Cucumber Spears with Citrus Vinaigrette

Cool as a cucumber, jicama tastes like a cross between a potato and an apple and is served raw, as in this refreshing snacky starter. It's perfect stand-around-and-munch food to set out while guests await the full-on feast. You can cut the cucumber and jicama up to two hours in advance; keep them in the refrigerator, wrapped in slightly damp paper towels.

- 1 teaspoon cumin seeds, plus more for serving
- ½ cup fresh orange juice
- 2 tablespoons fresh lemon juice
- 1 tablespoon extra-virgin olive oil
- 1 tablespoon honey
- 2 teaspoons Dijon mustard

  Pinch each of coarse salt and freshly ground pepper
- 4 large cucumbers, cut into ½-by-4-inch spears
- 2 jicamas, peeled and cut into ½-by-4-inch spears

  Ancho chile powder, for serving

1. Toast cumin seeds in a small skillet over medium-high heat until fragrant, about 2 minutes. Remove from heat; cool slightly. Transfer to a spice grinder and process until finely ground.

2. Whisk ground cumin, both juices, oil, honey, Dijon, and salt and pepper. (Store vinaigrette, covered, in the refrigerator up to 3 days.)

3. Toss cucumbers and jicama spears lightly with vinaigrette. Serve with additional vinaigrette on the side, as well as cumin seeds and chile powder, for sprinkling.

Frozen Fruit Pops

In the spirit of hands-on eating and drinking, offer pretty, portable, pastel pops for dessert. The treats could not be any simpler to prepare: Look for bottled fruit nectar in large supermarkets or at Latin groceries or bodegas. This yields 4 to 6 pops, depending on the size of the molds; make a few different fruit flavors, for variety.

- 2 cups fruit nectar, such as mango, pear, apricot, or banana
- ¼ cup heavy cream

Combine fruit nectar and cream in a blender and puree until smooth. Transfer to ice-pop molds and freeze.

FROZEN POPS

You don't have to be a kid to enjoy a frozen treat on a stick. They take down the heat, whether it comes from the weather or from a spicy meal—and they're just plain fun to eat. You can use fruit nectars, as in this recipe, to make them any time of the year. And in summer, when fresh fruits are plentiful, their juices are perfect for making vibrant pops. Puree berries, peaches, and plums; combine them with simple syrup (equal parts sugar and water brought to a boil and then cooled completely) and freeze. The base should taste a little too sweet before it's frozen, because the cold will mute the flavor. Store-bought yogurts, ice creams, gelatos, and sorbets can also fill molds, singly or in layers.

Experiment with shapes. Gelatin molds, yogurt containers, and waxed paper drinking cups will all yield nice results. The only rule is that the molds must be deep enough to secure the sticks.

SOLSTICE CELEBRATION

So many summer meals are casual and loose—picnics, clambakes, backyard barbecues, and such. That's why it can feel especially (and unexpectedly) lovely to set a nice table and sit down to a dinner that welcomes the season of longer days and magical nights, in style. SERVES 6

The Menu St-Germain, Gin, and Plum Cocktail ▪ Elderflower Spritz ▪ Roasted Apricots with Ricotta ▪ Chilled Cucumber, Yogurt, and Horseradish Soup ▪ Grilled-Salmon Salad ▪ Brown-Sugar Pavlova with Lemon Cream

St-Germain, Gin, and Plum Cocktail

Leave the pitcher of drinks behind and offer a couple of bespoke cocktails. This is perfect with thin slices of juicy plum, but feel free to swap in peaches or berries—or anything else that looks good at the market. Serve fresh radishes with butter and salt alongside, for dipping and sprinkling, and thinly sliced cucumbers, too.

1 ounce St-Germain (elderflower liqueur)
2 ounces gin
2 thin plum slices

Fill a cocktail shaker with ice. Add St-Germain and gin and shake vigorously. Strain into a glass, add plum slices, and serve.

Elderflower Spritz

1 ounce St-Germain (elderflower liqueur)
Vodka (optional)
Seltzer

Fill a small glass with ice. Pour St-Germain and vodka, if using, over ice. Top off with seltzer.

Roasted Apricots with Ricotta

You may think of fresh fruit only when it comes to dessert, breakfast, or an afternoon snack. Here, however, apricots take a detour toward the cocktail hour. They are halved and roasted with garlic and herbs, then topped with ricotta cheese for a knockout sweet-savory, not-too-heavy starter. They are delicious served a little warm from the oven or at room temperature.

12 apricots, halved and pitted
2 garlic cloves, thinly sliced
½ bunch thyme
½ bunch lavender
Extra-virgin olive oil
Coarse salt, preferably flaky sea salt, and freshly ground pepper
¾ cup fresh ricotta
Honey, for drizzling

Preheat oven to 425°F. Arrange apricot halves, cut-side up, on a parchment-lined rimmed baking sheet. Top with garlic, and thyme and lavender sprigs; drizzle with oil and sprinkle with salt and pepper. Roast until apricots are hot and juicy, about 15 minutes (no longer or the fruit will begin to fall apart). Dollop ricotta over apricots and drizzle with honey just before serving.

PREP PLAN

Two Days Before
Soft-boil eggs for salad

One Day Before
Prepare lemon curd

The Day Of
Bake pavlova and let cool

Boil potatoes, let cool, and halve; prepare anchovy dressing

Make and chill topping for pavlova

Chill serving bowls for soup

Just Before Guests Arrive
Make and chill cucumber soup (1 hour ahead); prep garnishes

Set out components for cocktails

Roast apricot halves

Heat grill (or grill pan); cook salmon and snap peas

Assemble pavlova

Chilled Cucumber, Yogurt, and Horseradish Soup

Step away from the stove: All you need to make this no-cook, 15-minute soup is a blender and a refrigerator. Yet the flavor is surprisingly complex. The secret is pairing mellow produce, creamy dairy, and a shot of something spicy—in this case, freshly grated horseradish (you could use prepared horseradish in its place).

4   small seedless cucumbers, plus more (thinly sliced), for garnish

3   cups low-fat plain yogurt

3   tablespoons finely grated lemon zest (from 3 to 4 lemons), plus strips of zest for garnish

2   tablespoons finely grated peeled fresh horseradish

    Freshly ground pepper

Cut cucumbers into large chunks. Puree half the cucumbers with yogurt, lemon zest, and horseradish in a blender until just smooth. Add remaining cucumber and pulse until chunky, about 4 times. Season with pepper. Refrigerate until cold, about 1 hour. Serve in chilled bowls, garnished with thinly sliced cucumber, lemon zest, and grated horseradish.

Grilled-Salmon Salad

A niçoise-inspired main-course salad (grilled salmon, six-minute eggs, fresh sugar snap peas, and boiled new potatoes) is dinner party—worthy, but especially so on an evening in early summer, with a bowlful of freshly made aïoli (go to marthastewart.com for a recipe). You can present the main components on a platter, as here, and serve lightly dressed watercress or other greens on the side. Or, toss everything into one large salad bowl; just flake the salmon into large pieces first and top the greens with the fish and the other ingredients just before serving.

8   anchovy fillets packed in olive oil, drained

1   teaspoon Dijon mustard

1   teaspoon finely grated lemon zest, plus 3 tablespoons fresh lemon juice (from 1 to 2 lemons)

½   cup extra-virgin olive oil, plus more for brushing

    Coarse salt and freshly ground pepper

12   ounces small new potatoes

1¼   pounds skin-on salmon fillet (about 1¾ inches at thickest part)

12   ounces sugar snap peas, trimmed

6   large eggs

6   cups baby greens, stems trimmed

1. Mash anchovies with a spoon in a small bowl. Add Dijon and 2 tablespoons lemon juice. Gradually whisk in oil. Season with salt and pepper and set aside.

2. In a large pot, cover potatoes with 2 inches water. Add 1 tablespoon salt. Bring to a boil, then reduce to a simmer and cook until knife-tender, about 12 minutes; drain. Let stand until cool enough to handle, then halve potatoes.

3. Heat grill (or grill pan) to medium-high (if using a charcoal grill, coals are ready when you can hold your hand 5 inches above grill for just 3 to 4 seconds). Brush salmon lightly with oil, sprinkle with zest and remaining tablespoon lemon juice, and season with salt and pepper. Brush grill grates with oil, then place salmon on grill, skin-side down. Cook until skin is crisp and browned, about 6 minutes a side for medium-rare, 8 minutes a side for medium. Remove from grill; transfer to a platter.

4. Meanwhile, bring a pot of water to a boil. Gently lower eggs into pot; simmer 6 minutes. Drain, then run under cold water to stop cooking; peel and halve.

5. Pour half of dressing into a serving bowl. Add potatoes and sugar snap peas; toss to coat. Add baby greens and toss again. Arrange potatoes, peas, greens, and eggs around salmon. Serve remaining dressing alongside.

Brown-Sugar Pavlova with Lemon Cream

Pavlova only sounds fancy. This heavenly dessert is little more than egg whites whipped with sugar, then baked into a crisp shell and topped with freshly whipped cream and fruit. There's nothing precise about it; a good amount of wonky imperfection only lends it more appeal. Use whatever fruit happens to be in season (red currants are shown, but it's wonderful with fresh berries, sliced peaches, or poached pears). The lemon curd here is also optional; feel free to leave it out and just top the whole thing with pure (insanely delicious) whipped cream. No one will turn down a second piece.

For meringue base

4	large egg whites
	Pinch of salt
¾	cup packed light-brown sugar
¼	cup superfine sugar
1	teaspoon distilled white vinegar
1	teaspoon pure vanilla extract

For topping

2	cups heavy cream
¼	cup superfine sugar
	Lemon Curd (recipe follows)
	Fresh red currants

1. Make meringue base: Place egg whites, salt, and brown sugar in the bowl of an electric mixer fitted with the whisk attachment. Beat on low speed until well combined and no lumps of sugar remain. Increase speed to medium; beat until soft peaks form, about 9 minutes. With mixer running, gradually add superfine sugar. Continue beating until peaks are stiff and glossy, about 2 minutes more. Beat in vinegar and vanilla.

2. Using a flexible spatula, spread meringue into 8-by-11-inch rectangle on a parchment-lined baking sheet; form a slight border of peaks around the edges and a shallow well in the center.

3. Bake meringue until crisp around the edges and just set in the center, about 1¼ hours. Transfer baking sheet to a wire rack until meringue is cool enough to handle. Carefully peel off parchment; let meringue cool completely on rack.

4. Make topping: In a small bowl, whip heavy cream and sugar until soft peaks form. Gently fold lemon curd into cream until streaked through (do not overmix). Cover with plastic wrap; refrigerate until ready to use.

5. To serve, carefully place meringue on platter. Spoon and spread lemon cream evenly over top, then top with currants.

LEMON CURD

1	large egg plus 3 large egg yolks
½	cup sugar
1½	teaspoons finely grated lemon zest plus ¼ cup plus 2 tablespoons fresh lemon juice (from 2 to 3 lemons)
	Pinch of salt
4	tablespoons unsalted butter, cut into pieces

In a saucepan, whisk together egg, yolks, sugar, lemon zest and juice, and salt. Bring to a simmer over medium heat, whisking constantly. Cook until mixture is thickened, 4 to 5 minutes. Strain through a fine sieve into a bowl. Whisk in butter, one piece at a time, until melted completely. Press plastic wrap directly onto surface of lemon curd and refrigerate until cold, at least 1 hour or up to overnight.

BACKYARD COOKOUT

Break free from burgers and hot dogs the next time you gather around the grill. This menu features bright Mediterranean flavors and favorites: fruit–filled cocktails and a meze platter to start things off, accompanied by lemony grilled lamb and chicken, tabbouleh salad, and warm flatbreads to wrap things up. **SERVES 10**

The Menu Mojitos with Basil and Summer Fruit ■ Tabbouleh ■ Grilled Flatbreads ■ Tzatziki ■ Grilled Marinated Leg of Lamb ■ Grilled Marinated Chicken ■ Peach-Pie Crumble Bars

PREP PLAN

One Week Before

Prepare syrup for mojitos

Preserve lemons (if not buying)

Three Days Before

Prepare fruit mixture for mojitos

Bake peach-pie crumble bars

One Day Before

Marinate lamb and chicken

Make tzatziki (whisk just before serving)

Prepare dough for flatbreads

A Few Hours Before Guests Arrive

Make tabbouleh (stir in mint just before serving)

Heat grill; bring lamb and chicken to room temperature

Just Before Guests Arrive

Grill vegetables, lamb, chicken, and flatbreads

Combine fruit mix and vodka and set out other components for mojitos

Mojitos with Basil and Summer Fruit

Any variety of summer fruits will do in this cocktail: You can even use an equal quantity of frozen ones, partially thawed with their juices. Serve it in a large pitcher or, as shown here, a wide-mouthed jar with a ladle. This recipe doubles easily.

½	cup plus 2 tablespoons sugar
1¼	cups water
⅓	cup fresh lemon juice
1½	pounds mixed summer fruit, such as sliced apricots, peaches, berries, or sour cherries
½	cup fresh basil leaves, plus more for serving
1½ to 2	cups vodka
3	cups sparkling water

1. Bring sugar and water to a boil in a small saucepan, stirring until sugar is dissolved, about 3 minutes. Remove from heat; let cool 15 minutes. (Syrup can be refrigerated for up to 1 week.)

2. Combine lemon juice, fruit, and basil in a bowl. Add syrup; mash lightly to release juices. Refrigerate at least 1 day and up to 4 days.

3. Combine fruit mixture and vodka in a pitcher; ladle about ⅓ cup into each glass. Fill with ice, top with sparkling water, and serve.

Tabbouleh

This Mediterranean restaurant favorite is often served as part of a meze platter, along with toasted flatbread and spreads like hummus and baba ghanoush. Tabbouleh is always a good choice for entertaining since it can be made ahead; cover and refrigerate up to 8 hours, but stir in the mint just before serving.

2	cups bulgur wheat
8	plum tomatoes, finely chopped, juices reserved
2¼	cups finely chopped fresh flat-leaf parsley (about 2 bunches)
8	scallions, trimmed and finely chopped
½	cup fresh lemon juice (from 3 to 4 lemons)
½	cup extra-virgin olive oil
	Coarse salt and freshly ground pepper
¼	cup finely chopped fresh mint

1. In a bowl, cover bulgur with cold water and soak for 10 minutes. Drain in a sieve lined with damp cheesecloth, then gather the cheesecloth and squeeze as much water as possible from the bulgur. Transfer to a serving bowl and fluff with a fork.

2. Stir in tomatoes and reserved juice, parsley, and scallions. Add lemon juice and oil, season with salt and pepper, and toss well. Stir in mint right before serving.

Grilled Flatbreads

Of course, you can just use store-bought flatbreads or large pita breads for meze, but making them from scratch is easy, and the process feels almost magical. It starts with a simple yeast dough (we used some whole-wheat flour in addition to white) that gets "baked" over a very hot grill. The heat activates the yeast and creates steam, which causes the dough to puff up dramatically, forming the signature pocket. Serve half the flatbreads as an appetizer with spinach, yogurt, and toasted sesame seeds alongside stuffed grape leaves, feta, olives, and tzatziki, and save the rest to serve with the lamb and chicken. This recipe yields 16 breads.

4½	cups all-purpose flour, plus more for dusting
2	envelopes (¼ ounce each) active dry yeast (4½ teaspoons)
1	tablespoon honey
2¼	cups warm water (110°F)
1½	cups whole-wheat flour
1	tablespoon coarse salt
⅓	cup extra-virgin olive oil, plus more for bowl
	Fine cornmeal, for sprinkling

1. In a large bowl, whisk together 1 cup all-purpose flour, the yeast, honey, and 1 cup warm water until smooth. Cover with plastic wrap; let rise in a warm spot until doubled in bulk, about 30 minutes. Stir in remaining 3½ cups all-purpose flour, the whole-wheat flour, salt, oil, and remaining 1¼ cups warm water.

2. Transfer dough to a lightly floured work surface. Knead, dusting hands and work surface with more flour as needed, until smooth and elastic, about 10 minutes. Transfer to a large oiled bowl, turning to coat. Cover and let rise again until doubled in bulk, about 45 minutes.

3. Punch down dough and form into a ball, then turn out onto lightly floured surface. Quarter dough. Working with 1 piece at a time (drape a kitchen towel over the rest), divide each into 4 smaller pieces. Roll each piece into a ball and pinch, tightening ball. Turn pinched-side down and flatten with your palm.

4. Flatten each ball into a 6-inch round with a lightly floured rolling pin. Transfer rounds to rimmed baking sheets sprinkled with cornmeal; drape with kitchen towels. Let stand 30 minutes. (Dough can be refrigerated up to 2 days.)

5. Heat grill (or grill pan) to medium-high (if using a charcoal grill, coals are ready when you can hold your hand 5 inches above grill for just 3 to 4 seconds). Working in batches and using tongs, place rounds directly on grill and cook until dough bubbles and puffs, 3 to 4 minutes, then flip and grill other side until blackened in spots and cooked through, about 2 minutes more. Transfer to a basket lined with a kitchen towel; cover to steam and keep warm. Grill remaining flatbreads. (Flatbread is best served the same day but can be kept in an airtight container at room temperature for up to 1 day.)

Tzatziki

To avoid a waterlogged sauce, wrap the grated cucumber in paper towels and give it a good squeeze to remove excess moisture. You can also place it in a colander over the sink and press gently.

2	medium cucumbers, seeded, coarsely grated, and squeezed of excess moisture
1	cup plain yogurt, preferably Greek
¼	cup chopped fresh flat-leaf parsley
2 to 4	tablespoons fresh lemon juice
	Coarse salt and freshly ground pepper

In a small bowl, combine cucumbers, yogurt, parsley, and lemon juice to taste. Season with salt and pepper and serve. (Can be made 1 day in advance; refrigerate and whisk before serving.)

GRILLING VEGETABLES 101

Get in the habit of throwing some vegetables on the grill whenever it's fired up. They make a great side for whatever you're serving, and having a bunch of them on the table allows plenty of options for vegetarians. Brush vegetables on all sides with olive oil, and season with coarse salt and freshly ground pepper before grilling.

Eggplant
Cut lengthwise into ½-inch-thick slices, season, and grill over medium-high about 3 minutes, until golden and marked in spots; then flip and transfer to medium heat for 5 to 6 minutes.

Zucchini and Summer Squash
Cut into ¼-inch lengthwise slices, season, and grill over medium-high until marked and tender, 3 to 4 minutes each side.

Bell Peppers
Season whole peppers and grill, turning continuously over high heat until charred, 15 to 18 minutes. Steam in a bowl covered with plastic wrap for 10 minutes to remove skins, if desired.

Red and Yellow Onions
Cut onions into ½-inch pieces, keeping rings intact, and thread onto skewers. Season and grill over low heat, about 15 minutes, then flip and grill until cooked through, 15 to 18 minutes more.

HOW TO SET UP THE GRILL

Here's the key to grilling success, whether with a gas or a charcoal grill: Create two zones—one for high, direct heat for searing and another for low, indirect heat for cooking the meat through.

Preparing a Charcoal Grill
Start with hardwood lump charcoal instead of briquettes. It's free of chemical additives and it burns hotter and longer. A chimney starter is preferable to a liquid fire starter, which can impart a chemical taste to food. Once lit, use long-handled tongs to rearrange the charcoal, leaving a third of the grill free of charcoal (this will be the indirect-heat zone). Leave the lid off when the grill is heating. When you put the lid on for indirect cooking, leave the air vents open to allow airflow.

Preparing a Gas Grill
Turn all the burners on high, cover, and heat for 15 minutes. Turn off one of the burners, creating your indirect-heat zone. Adjust the remaining burners to medium-high.

Checking Temperature
With a charcoal grill, hold the palm of your hand carefully over the charcoal, where the food would be. If you can hold your hand there for just 3 to 4 seconds, it's medium-high heat.

Grilled Marinated Leg of Lamb

This marinade does double duty: Some of it flavors the lamb and chicken before grilling, and the rest is reserved to serve alongside. It's heady with the tastes and incredible aromas of preserved lemons, garlic, red chiles, fresh mint, and marjoram.

2	preserved lemons
10	garlic cloves, chopped
2	shallots, chopped
4	small dried red chiles, stemmed and crumbled (about 2 teaspoons)
2	cups fresh mint leaves, plus sprigs for serving
½	cup fresh marjoram leaves, plus sprigs for serving
	Juice and grated zest of 2 lemons, plus lemon halves for serving
1	teaspoon coarse salt
2	cups extra-virgin olive oil
3	pounds boneless leg of lamb, butterflied and pounded to an even thickness (1 to 1½ inches)

1. Halve preserved lemons; remove and discard seeds and flesh. Chop skin and pulse with garlic, shallot, chiles, mint and marjoram leaves, lemon zest and juice, and salt in a food processor until coarsely ground. Stir in oil. Reserve 2 cups marinade (1 cup for chicken and 1 cup for serving).

2. Place lamb in a baking pan; rub with marinade. Refrigerate, covered, overnight.

3. Let lamb stand at room temperature 1 hour. Heat grill (or grill pan) to medium-high (see sidebar). Remove lamb from marinade, brushing off excess. Grill, covered, 8 minutes. Flip; continue cooking until a thermometer inserted

in center reads 130°F for medium-rare, about 8 minutes more. Remove from grill and cover loosely with foil; let rest 20 minutes. Slice thinly and serve with herb sprigs, lemon halves, and reserved marinade.

Grilled Marinated Chicken

To ensure moist chicken, keep a close eye on the meat as it cooks and use an instant-read thermometer. Marinades help, but the chicken will dry out fast (especially the breasts) after reaching an internal temperature of 165°F.

1	whole chicken (3 to 4 pounds), cut into 10 pieces (breasts halved on the diagonal)
1	cup reserved preserved lemon marinade (see previous recipe)
	Safflower or other vegetable oil, for brushing

1. Place chicken parts in a baking pan. Toss with marinade, turning to coat. Refrigerate for at least 4 hours or overnight, turning chicken occasionally. Remove chicken from refrigerator 30 minutes before grilling.

2. Heat grill (or grill pan) to medium with direct and indirect heat zones (see sidebar). Brush grates with oil. Remove chicken from marinade and pat dry with paper towels. Grill breast halves, thighs, and drumsticks, skin-side down, over direct heat for 10 minutes.

3. Flip, move to indirect heat, and grill, covered, until an instant-read thermometer inserted into the thickest part of thighs registers 165°F, 10 to 15 minutes. Grill wings over direct heat, flipping often, until cooked through, about 15 minutes. Serve with additional reserved marinade on the side.

Peach-Pie Crumble Bars

With a press-in shortbread crust that doubles as a topping, peach pie becomes fuss-free (and fork-free to boot). Another bonus: Lining the pan with parchment makes removing the bars a breeze.

For crust

- ½ cup (1 stick) plus 5 tablespoons unsalted butter, room temperature, plus more for pan
- 1 cup sugar
- 2 cups all-purpose flour
- 1 teaspoon coarse salt

For filling

- 1¼ pounds peaches, pitted and cut into ½-inch dice (3½ cups)
- ½ cup sugar
- 2 tablespoons all-purpose flour
- 1 tablespoon fresh lemon juice
- ½ teaspoon coarse salt

1. Preheat oven to 375°F. Butter an 8-by-8-by-2-inch baking pan. Line with parchment, leaving a 2-inch overhang on two sides; butter parchment.

2. Make crust: With an electric mixer, beat butter and sugar in a bowl until light and fluffy, about 3 minutes. Scrape down bowl. Add flour and salt; beat just until dough forms clumps but does not completely hold together. Press 2½ cups flour mixture into bottom and 1 inch up sides of prepared pan. Reserve the remainder.

3. Make filling: Stir together peaches, sugar, flour, lemon juice, and salt in a bowl. Pour into crust. Crumble remaining flour mixture evenly over top, squeezing to create clumps. Bake until bubbling in center and crust is golden, about 1 hour 10 minutes (if browning too quickly, tent top with foil). Let cool in pan, about 1 hour. Refrigerate, wrapped tightly in plastic or in an airtight container, until ready to serve (up to 3 days). Cut into squares and serve.

GRILLED FRUIT

If you're looking for a simple finale for a backyard dinner (and you don't feel like turning on the oven), consider grilling some fruit. The heat of the grill deepens the natural sweetness and turns just about any fresh fruit into a wonderful dessert.

Grilled stone fruits take on a satisfying, smoky finish: Halve and pit peaches, plums, nectarines, or apricots; drizzle with olive oil; and grill, cut-side down, until juicy and charred, 2 to 4 minutes.

Slice peeled and cored pineapple into rounds, or cut a mango or melon into large wedges; brush fruit pieces with melted butter or olive oil and grill just until browned on both sides.

Serve grilled fruit over ice cream with caramel sauce (recipe on page 267), or top with fresh whipped cream and crumbled gingersnaps. Or try it as a topping for grilled angel food or pound cake. Finishing with a light drizzle of aged balsamic vinegar will complement the sweetness.

The Menu Albariño Sangria Spritz Cocktails ▪ Sherry with Olives ▪ Pan Tomate ▪ Roasted Dried Figs ▪ Charred Leeks with Romesco ▪ Paella ▪ Olive-Oil Cake with Whipped Cream and Brandied Cherries

Albariño Sangria Spritz Cocktails

Bright, zesty, crisp white Albariño is an especially nice choice for sangria, especially if you are eating outside on a warm summer night.

- 1   bottle (750 milliliters) Albariño, chilled
- 1   cup Cointreau (or other orange liqueur)
- 1   lime, thinly sliced
- 1   lemon, thinly sliced
- 1   orange, thinly sliced
- 3   cups seltzer, chilled

Stir together wine, Cointreau, lime, lemon, and orange. Divide among ice-filled glasses. Top each with seltzer.

Sherry with Olives

For those who don't like sangria (hard to believe, but such people do exist), here's another drink from Spain that pairs perfectly with tapas and paella.

- 1   bottle (750 milliliters) dry sherry, such as fino or manzanilla, chilled
- 1   jar (5 ounces) Spanish olives, pitted (plain or stuffed with pimientos, almonds, or garlic)

Pour sherry into small glasses, add 2 or 3 olives to each, and serve.

SANGRIA 101

One of the ultimate good-time drinks of summer, sangria is, at its heart, a blend of wine, fruit, seltzer, and sometimes brandy. It's a drink built for variation: Some sangrias include fruit-flavored liqueurs; others call for fruit juices. Sangria is most often made with red wine, but, as in this recipe, those made with white, rosé, or sparkling wines are just as delicious.

Although sangria was originally made with Rioja wine, you can use just about any dry red wine. Other (non-Spanish) good choices include Beaujolais, Pinot Noir, and Sangiovese. For white sangria, try dry white wines such as Albariño, Pinot Grigio, or Sauvignon Blanc.

Chill the bottle of wine thoroughly before using; this will help prevent the ice from melting too quickly in the glass and diluting the taste. To allow the flavors to blend, make and refrigerate the punch up to a day ahead of time, adding ice and seltzer just before serving.

Pan Tomate

One of the simplest and best-known tapas is *pan tomate*, or tomato bread. It's delicious all on its own, but it also makes a great vehicle for a few more substantial pre-dinner snacks, like Serrano ham, or the white anchovies known as boquerones; both are widely available exports from Spain. Other nice additions are Cabrales (a Spanish blue cheese), and Roasted Dried Figs (recipe follows).

1	baguette, cut into 24 (½-inch) slices
¼	cup olive oil
2	garlic cloves, cut in half lengthwise
4	Roma tomatoes
	Coarse salt
	Serrano ham, thinly sliced, for serving
	Boquerones, drained, patted dry, and halved lengthwise, for serving

1. Preheat oven to 400°F. Lay bread slices on a rimmed baking sheet and brush cut sides with oil. Toast until lightly golden brown, 8 to 10 minutes. Rub each piece of bread with the cut side of a garlic clove.
2. Grate tomatoes on the large holes of a grater, discarding the skins. Season with salt. Spoon 1 teaspoon tomato over each piece of bread. Arrange a small slice of ham or a boquerone over tomato and serve.

Roasted Dried Figs

Roasting brings out the richness in these bite-size salty-sweet flavor bombs. Any dried fig will do; the two most common varieties are Black Mission and Turkish.

2	tablespoons extra-virgin olive oil, plus more for baking sheet
1	tablespoon honey
1	pound dried figs, halved if large
4	sprigs thyme
½	teaspoon flaky salt, such as Maldon

1. Preheat oven to 400°F. Lightly brush a rimmed baking sheet with oil. Whisk oil and honey in a large bowl. Add figs; toss to coat.

2. Arrange figs in a single layer on prepared sheet and scatter thyme sprigs on top. Sprinkle with salt. Roast until fragrant and caramelized, 12 to 15 minutes, tossing halfway through. Let figs cool slightly before serving.

Charred Leeks with Romesco

Romesco sauce is a Catalonian classic with a nutty texture and a flavor made earthy with charred red peppers and smoked paprika. It's a great dip for vegetables as well as a sauce served alongside grilled chicken, meat, or fish.

2	red bell peppers
1	small garlic clove, smashed
½	cup blanched almonds, toasted
1	tablespoon sherry vinegar
1	tablespoon tomato paste
1	teaspoon hot smoked paprika
½	cup plus 2 tablespoons extra-virgin olive oil
	Coarse salt and freshly ground pepper
6	large leeks, stems trimmed but attached, halved lengthwise and rinsed well

1. Char peppers over the flame of a gas stove, turning with tongs, until blackened and blistered. (Or char under broiler on a rimmed baking sheet, turning as needed.) Transfer to a bowl, cover with a plate, and let steam 15 minutes. Remove skins, using paper towels (and a paring knife for any stubborn spots); discard. Remove and discard stems, ribs, and seeds.

2. Transfer peppers to a food processor. Add garlic, almonds, vinegar, tomato paste, and pimentón. Pulse until combined. With machine running, slowly add oil, processing until combined. Season with salt. (Romesco can be refrigerated in an airtight container for up to 3 days; serve at room temperature.)

3. Heat grill pan over medium-high. Brush leeks with oil and season with salt and pepper. Grill in 3 batches, flipping every few minutes until leeks are charred in places and soft, about 10 minutes per batch. Transfer to a platter and serve with a bowl of romesco.

Paella

You may be tempted to grab any old short-grained rice to make paella, but treat yourself to Spanish Bomba rice, which absorbs liquid and flavors without getting sticky. And speaking of treats, don't forget the saffron, whose prized slender threads are essential to this Spanish national treasure.

4	cups low-sodium chicken broth	5	garlic cloves, minced
	Large pinch of saffron	2	teaspoons sweet smoked paprika
3	tablespoons extra-virgin olive oil	2¼	cups short-grained rice, such as Bomba
12	ounces bone-in skin-on chicken thighs	¼	cup dry white wine
	Flaky salt, such as Maldon, and freshly ground pepper	½	pound squid (tubes and tentacles)
4	ounces chorizo, sliced ⅓-inch thick	½	pound medium shrimp, cleaned and deveined but not peeled
2	medium onions, quartered and thinly sliced	1	pound mussels, scrubbed
1	small leek, well rinsed and sliced	1	pound littleneck clams, scrubbed
		½	cup fresh or frozen peas

1. In a small saucepan, heat chicken broth and saffron over low; cover and let steep 15 minutes.

2. Heat a 15-inch paella pan or a wide, shallow skillet over medium-high. Coat the bottom of pan with oil. Season chicken with salt and pepper, and add chicken, skin-side down, to hot pan. Cook, turning once, until browned, 5 to 7 minutes. Add chorizo; cook, moving chicken to sides to make room, until browned and fat is rendered, about 3 minutes. Add onions, leek, garlic, paprika, and 1 teaspoon salt. Season generously with pepper, and cook, stirring, until soft.

3. Add rice to pan and stir to coat. Add wine and let cook about 1 minute. Add chicken-saffron broth; season with salt. Add seafood and bring to a boil (once seafood is added, let mixture sit; do not stir or mix). After 5 minutes, add peas; cook—without stirring—until rice is tender, shellfish has opened, and nearly all liquid has evaporated and bubbles have thickened, 15 to 20 minutes. Serve paella immediately.

PAELLA PANS You can make paella easily in a wide, shallow skillet, but if this Valencian classic turns up regularly on your dinner party menu, you may want to invest in a paella pan. Traditionally made of carbon steel (but also available in stainless or enameled steel), the pan's shallow, sloped sides and wide bottom enable the rice and seafood dish to cook evenly and encourage a caramelized crust (called *socarrat*) to form. Wide handles let you carry the dish from stovetop to table for serving.

BUYING SHELLFISH

Clams
Choose live clams with tightly closed shells. If the shells are slightly open, tap them. Discard any that don't close immediately. They should smell of the ocean, nothing more.

Mussels
Don't bother buying mussels with chipped or damaged shells. Before cooking, clean and debeard them: Holding mussels under cool running water, scrub with a stiff sponge (or vegetable brush). Then grip the tough fibers extending from the shell—the beard—and pull to remove them; discard beards.

Shrimp
Fresh or frozen shrimp are equally good picks, as most boats flash-freeze the shrimp on board. But shrimp still in the shell can be tastier and less expensive. Thaw frozen shrimp in the refrigerator for one to two days or, in a pinch, run them under cold water. Chill fresh shrimp for up to two days. If the shrimp is farmed, look for the Best Aquaculture Practices label. For wild shrimp, look for certification from Wild American Shrimp or the Marine Stewardship Council.

PREP PLAN

One Week Before

Prepare brandied cherries

Two to Three Days Before

Prepare romesco sauce

Bake cake

Chill wine for sangria

One Day Before

Mix chilled wine and the
Cointreau for sangria; chill
punch, sherry, and seltzer

The Day Of

Prep ingredients for paella

Toast baguette slices
and rub with garlic

Bring romesco to room
temperature

Whip cream for dessert

Just Before Guests Arrive

Heat grill (or grill pan);
grill leeks

Finish pan tomate
with toppings

Roast figs

Stir together sangria
in a pitcher

Cook paella

Olive-Oil Cake with Whipped Cream and Brandied Cherries

Lots of Spanish desserts include olive oil rather than butter. This one is very similar in flavor to the thin, flaky biscuits known as *tortas de aceite*, but with a cakey, tender crumb. Serve with unsweetened whipped cream and brandied cherries, as suggested below, or top with whipped cream and fresh cherries or sliced fresh peaches or apricots.

1	cup extra-virgin olive oil, plus more for brushing
1⅓	cups cake flour (not self-rising), plus more for the pan
4	large eggs plus 2 large egg yolks
1	cup sugar, plus more for sprinkling
2	packed teaspoons finely grated orange zest (from 1 orange)
1	tablespoon anise seeds
1	teaspoon coarse salt
1	teaspoon baking powder
1	cup heavy cream, for serving
	Brandied Cherries (recipe follows), for serving

1. Preheat oven to 350°F. Lightly brush an 8-inch round pan with oil and dust with flour, tapping out excess. Whisk eggs, yolks, sugar, orange zest, and 2 teaspoons anise seeds in a bowl until foamy. Add oil in a slow, steady stream, whisking constantly until combined.

2. Whisk flour, salt, and baking powder in a small bowl. Fold into egg mixture in 3 additions. Pour batter into pan, sprinkle with sugar and remaining teaspoon anise seeds, and bake until lightly golden and a tester inserted into center comes out clean, 35 to 40 minutes. Let cool in pan for 10 minutes. Turn out cake onto wire rack and let cool completely; reinvert cake onto serving platter.

3. In a chilled bowl, whip heavy cream until soft peaks form. Serve cake with brandied cherries and whipped cream.

BRANDIED CHERRIES

1¼	pounds frozen sweet cherries, partially thawed
¼	cup fresh lemon juice
¼	cup sugar
¼	teaspoon salt
¼	cup brandy

In a saucepan over medium-high heat, bring cherries, lemon juice, sugar, and salt to a boil. Reduce heat and simmer 5 minutes. Remove from heat and stir in brandy. Return to heat and simmer 1 minute more. Let cool completely. (Cherries can be refrigerated in an airtight container for up to 2 weeks.)

PASTA NIGHT

Comfort food, Italian–style, means dishing up platters of tender pasta topped with a choice of familiar sauces: rich, meaty, long-simmered Bolognese or bright, pungent pesto Genovese. Start with a few classic cocktails and a fresher take on antipasti (more vegetables, fewer meats), and end with the winning combination of biscotti, pignoli cookies, and affogato. **SERVES 8**

The Menu Negroni ▪ Aperol Spritz ▪ Marinated Artichokes ▪ Garlic Bread ▪ Poached Tomatoes ▪ Romano Beans with Pancetta ▪ Arugula, Walnut, and Parmesan Salad ▪ Pasta Bolognese ▪ Pesto Genovese ▪ Pignoli Cookies ▪ Chocolate-Pistachio Biscotti ▪ Affogato

Negroni

This beloved Italian aperitif is a mix of gin, vermouth, and Campari. Legend has it that the ruby-hued drink was developed in the early twentieth century for Camillo Negroni. He was an Italian count who, according to one story, picked up a taste for British gin while traveling in England to indulge his passion for horse racing.

- 1 ounce gin
- 1 ounce sweet vermouth
- 1 ounce Campari
- 1 wide strip orange zest, for garnish

In a cocktail shaker filled with ice, combine gin, sweet vermouth, and Campari. Shake and strain into an ice-filled glass. Garnish with orange zest.

Aperol Spritz

Think of Aperol, a bitter-orange-and-rhubarb flavored aperitif, as a lighter, sweeter Campari. Pair it with prosecco and soda water for a bubbly, refreshing pre-dinner sip.

- 2 ounces Aperol
- 3 ounces prosecco

  Soda water, chilled

  Orange slice, for garnish

Fill an old-fashioned glass with ice. Add Aperol, prosecco, and soda water to fill. Garnish with orange slice.

Marinated Artichokes

In a pinch, you can always add store-bought marinated artichokes to a platter of antipasti, but these taste so much better. And if you've never tried baby artichokes, you are in for a treat. They don't require the same prep as full-size globe artichokes—simply remove the tough outer leaves and the stems, and scoop out the fuzzy chokes.

- 2 pounds baby artichokes
- 1 shallot, minced
- 2 tablespoons Dijon mustard
- ⅓ cup white-wine vinegar
- ¾ cup plus 2 tablespoons extra-virgin olive oil

  Coarse salt and freshly ground pepper

  Thyme sprigs, for garnish

1. Bring a large pot of salted water to a boil over high heat. Meanwhile, remove tough outer leaves and trim stems from artichokes. Slice them in half lengthwise and cut away the purple chokes; discard. Transfer artichokes to boiling water. Reduce heat and gently simmer until just tender, 5 to 7 minutes. Transfer artichokes to a colander using a slotted spoon.

2. In a bowl, whisk together shallot, mustard, and vinegar, and add oil in a slow, steady stream, whisking until emulsified. Season with salt and pepper. Add artichokes, tossing to combine. Serve, garnished with thyme. (Artichokes can be refrigerated in an airtight container up to 1 week.)

Garlic Bread

This Italian restaurant favorite gets a nice bit of vibrant color and flavor from butter mixed with chopped parsley—and lots of minced garlic, of course. The butter mixture is also delicious on steamed vegetables.

6	tablespoons unsalted butter, room temperature
4	garlic cloves, minced
¼	cup finely chopped fresh flat-leaf parsley
1	loaf rustic Italian bread, sliced crosswise (but not all the way through) at 1-inch intervals
	Coarse salt

Preheat oven to 350°F. Combine butter, garlic, and parsley in a bowl. Spread butter mixture evenly on cut sides of bread and sprinkle with salt. Wrap loaf loosely in aluminum foil. Bake until heated through and just beginning to crisp, about 20 minutes. Serve immediately.

Poached Tomatoes

Another nice addition to the antipasto platter, this is more of a technique than a recipe. The flavor of the tomatoes becomes more concentrated and deeply sweet as they roast. And don't discard the poaching oil afterward; you can use it in dressings and vinaigrettes, brush it over crostini or croutons, or toss it with warm pasta.

1	pound cherry tomatoes, preferably still on the vine
3	garlic cloves
	Extra-virgin olive oil

Place tomatoes and garlic in a small saucepan. Add enough oil to submerge tomatoes halfway, about 1¾ cups. Heat over low and gently poach tomatoes until very tender and almost falling apart, about 30 minutes. Serve room temperature tomatoes with antipasto; reserve oil for another use. (Poached tomatoes can be refrigerated in oil up to a week.)

Romano Beans with Pancetta

The Romano, or Italian flat bean, is hearty and meaty and stands up to longer cooking times but tastes best when it's crisp–tender. Romanos are in season from July to September, and can be found beside regular green beans at farmers' markets and grocery stores.

1	teaspoon extra-virgin olive oil
4	ounces sliced pancetta, cut into 1-inch pieces
1	pound Romano beans
	Coarse salt and freshly ground pepper
½	cup water

In a large skillet, heat oil over medium. Add pancetta and cook until crisp, about 10 minutes. Transfer pancetta to a small bowl and drain all but 2 teaspoons fat from skillet. Add beans to skillet, and season with salt and pepper. Add water, cover, and cook until beans are crisp-tender, about 4 minutes. Transfer beans to a platter and top with pancetta. Serve warm.

Arugula, Walnut, and Parmesan Salad

The Parmesan in this salad is sliced instead of grated or shaved for a more interesting texture—and flavor. Get in the habit of seasoning salads as you go instead of following a recipe for dressing. This way you will learn how you and your partner prefer them (more lemony, say, or peppery), and soon you will be tossing them without any need for a recipe at all.

2	bunches arugula, washed well and drained
1	small red onion, thinly sliced
⅓	cup walnuts, toasted and coarsely chopped
2	ounces Parmigiano-Reggiano cheese, thinly sliced
1	lemon, halved, plus more for serving
¼	cup extra-virgin olive oil, plus more for serving
	Coarse salt and freshly ground pepper

Place arugula on a long platter or in a large salad bowl. Top with onion, walnuts, and sliced cheese, distributing evenly. Before serving, squeeze lemon over salad, then drizzle with oil and sprinkle with salt and pepper. Toss salad together lightly, taste, and season with additional lemon juice, oil, salt, and pepper.

Pasta Bolognese

This sauce, named for the Italian city of Bologna in the Emilia-Romagna region, is decidedly hearty but also strikingly elegant. It's more than simply meat sauce. Instead, the combination of ground meats and diced vegetables is simmered with milk and red wine for a wonderfully rich flavor.

- 4 ounces pancetta, cut into 1/4-inch dice
- 3 onions, finely chopped
- 3 garlic cloves, finely chopped
- 3 carrots, finely chopped
- 3 stalks celery, finely chopped
- 1 pound ground beef, such as chuck or sirloin
- 1 pound ground pork
  Coarse salt and freshly ground pepper
- 2 cups dry red wine
- 2 cups milk
- 1 can (28 ounces) crushed tomatoes

1. In a large heavy-bottomed pan, cook pancetta over medium heat until golden and fat has rendered, 8 to 10 minutes. Add onions and garlic, and sauté until translucent, about 8 minutes (reduce heat if mixture is browning too quickly). Add carrots and celery, and cook until just beginning to soften, about 3 minutes.

2. Add beef and pork, and season with salt and pepper. Continue to cook over medium heat, stirring frequently and breaking up meat with a wooden spoon, until no longer pink, 8 to 10 minutes. Once meat is completely browned, pour off any excess fat. Add wine and raise heat to medium-high; cook, stirring to scrape up browned bits from bottom of pan, until liquid has evaporated, 10 to 12 minutes.

3. Add milk and cook until liquid has reduced by half, 6 to 8 minutes (don't worry if it appears slightly curdled at any point; it will smooth out again). Add tomatoes and bring to a boil. Reduce heat to low and simmer 12 to 15 minutes, until sauce has slightly thickened; the finished sauce should have the consistency of a loose chili. Season with salt and pepper. (If not serving immediately, let cool completely before transferring to airtight containers. Refrigerate up to 3 days or freeze up to 3 months; defrost overnight in the refrigerator before using.)

Pesto Genovese

Pesto was once considered an Italian delicacy, but today it is everywhere on the American table—and not just on pasta. Below is a recipe for the classic version, but like many good recipes, this one takes well to experimentation and improvisation. If you prefer, use walnuts or almonds in place of the pine nuts. You can also replace half the basil with arugula, parsley, or mint leaves.

- 2 garlic cloves
- 1/2 cup toasted pine nuts (see page 259)
- 8 cups fresh basil leaves (about 6 ounces)
- 1 cup extra-virgin olive oil, plus more for pouring over top (optional)
- 1 cup finely grated Parmigiano-Reggiano (4 ounces)
  Coarse salt and freshly ground pepper

In a food processor, pulse garlic and pine nuts until coarsely chopped. Add basil and 2 tablespoons oil, and process to combine. With machine running, add remaining oil in a slow, steady stream. Add Parmesan and pulse to combine. Season with salt and pepper. (To store, transfer to an airtight container, pour a thin layer of oil over the top of pesto, and refrigerate up to 1 week, or freeze for up to 3 months; defrost overnight in the refrigerator before using.)

Pignoli Cookies

These treats are a specialty at old-school Italian bakeries and cafes. The fact that they are gluten-free makes them that much more appealing to a bunch of dinner guests with mixed tastes and eating habits. We recommend serving the cookies with some store-bought torrone or other Italian confections.

1¼   cups whole pine nuts, plus 1 cup more, coarsely chopped, for rolling

1   cup whole raw almonds

½   cup granulated sugar

1   teaspoon finely grated orange zest

¼   teaspoon salt

3   large egg whites

½   teaspoon pure vanilla extract

Fine sanding sugar, for sprinkling

1. Preheat oven to 325°F. Spread 1¼ cups pine nuts and the almonds in a single layer on separate rimmed baking sheets. Toast, tossing occasionally, until fragrant and golden brown, about 8 minutes for pine nuts and 10 minutes for almonds. Let cool.

2. Combine nuts. Process half in a food processor with 3 tablespoons granulated sugar until finely ground. Transfer to a large bowl. Repeat with remaining nuts and 3 more tablespoons sugar, and add to bowl. Stir in orange zest and salt.

3. With an electric mixer, beat 2 egg whites until fluffy. Gradually add remaining 2 tablespoons sugar and vanilla, and beat until stiff peaks form. Fold into nut mixture (dough will be sticky).

4. Shape dough into 1½-inch balls and roll in chopped pine nuts. Transfer to parchment-lined rimmed baking sheets. Brush tops with remaining egg white and sprinkle with sanding sugar.

5. Bake until edges are golden and centers are set, 17 to 20 minutes. Let cool on sheets for 10 minutes, then transfer cookies to wire racks to cool completely. (Cookies can be stored in an airtight container for up to 3 days.)

Chocolate-Pistachio Biscotti

Crunchy, chocolaty, twice-baked cookies are great for dunking in milk or coffee. Almonds, peanuts, or hazelnuts would also work well in place of the pistachios.

2   cups all-purpose flour

1   cup sugar

1½   teaspoons baking powder

¼   teaspoon salt

¾   cup shelled unsalted pistachios

4   ounces dark chocolate, finely chopped

3   large eggs

2   tablespoons unsalted butter, melted

1   teaspoon pure vanilla extract

¼   cup unsweetened cocoa powder

1. Preheat oven to 350°F. In a large bowl, whisk together flour, ¾ cup sugar, baking powder, and salt; stir in pistachios and chocolate. In a small bowl, whisk together eggs, butter, vanilla, and cocoa. Add egg mixture to flour mixture and stir until combined (dough will be stiff, so mix with hands if necessary).

2. Line a rimmed baking sheet with parchment and sprinkle with 2 tablespoons sugar. Divide dough in half and place on sheet. Using wet hands, shape dough into two 2½-by-12-inch logs and sprinkle top of each with 1 tablespoon sugar. Bake until risen and firm, 15 to 20 minutes. Let logs cool completely on sheet, about 30 minutes.

3. Reduce oven to 300°F. Using a serrated knife, cut logs crosswise into ½-inch-thick slices. Arrange slices cut side down in a single layer on sheets. Bake until biscotti are dry, 15 to 20 minutes. Transfer to a wire rack to cool completely. (Keep in an airtight container at room temperature, up to 1 week.)

Affogato

This espresso-and-gelato concoction—*affogato* means "drowned" in Italian—serves as an after-dinner drink and a dessert in one. Vanilla ice cream is pictured, but use any flavor you like.

2   cups ice cream or gelato

1½   cups strong espresso

Arrange 8 small glasses on a rimmed baking sheet. Fill each with ¼ cup ice cream. Freeze until firm, about 30 minutes. Pour 3 tablespoons hot espresso over each. Serve immediately.

OCTOBER FEAST

In the spirit of the season, offer a spread of sausages, sauerkraut, pickles, and pretzels, with a selection of German beers. This is among the fastest parties to prep, since there's so little cooking involved. It's more about buying and assembling great ingredients, then kicking back to celebrate the autumn harvest. **SERVES 8**

The Menu Flammeküche ■ Quick-Pickled Vegetables ■
German Sausages with Apples, Sauerkraut, and
Onion ■ Warm Potato Salad with Arugula ■ Pretzel-Crust Ice
Cream Pie with Caramel Bourbon Sauce

Flammeküche

Serve this rich Alsatian bacon-and-onion tart with
a few bowls of Quick-Pickled Vegetables (recipe follows)
for a study in contrasts. For wine drinkers, try pairing
the starter (the whole meal, in fact) with Gewürztraminer
or a dry Alsatian Riesling.

	Cornmeal or semolina, for baking sheet
1	small onion, very thinly sliced
¼	cup plus 2 tablespoons heavy cream
4	slices bacon, cut crosswise into ¼-inch pieces
	Pinch of freshly grated nutmeg
1	pound pizza dough, homemade or store-bought
	All-purpose flour, for surface
	Coarse salt

1. Place a pizza stone on the lowest rack in oven. Preheat
oven to 500°F. Dust a baking sheet with cornmeal. Stir together
onion, cream, bacon, and nutmeg in a bowl.

2. Turn out dough onto a lightly floured work surface. Roll into an
irregular 12-by-18-inch rectangle. Place on prepared baking sheet.
Spread onion mixture evenly over dough, leaving a 1-inch border.
Drizzle with any cream remaining in bowl; season with salt.

3. Place sheet on stone in oven. Bake until bottom and
edges of dough are golden brown, 10 to 12 minutes. Cut into
squares and serve.

Quick-Pickled Vegetables

You can substitute two small fennel bulbs for the green
beans; just cut them into ¾-inch wedges.

3	cups cider vinegar
1	cup plus 2 tablespoons sugar
1½	teaspoons coarse salt
1½	teaspoons whole coriander seeds
¾	teaspoon whole fennel seeds
3	dried bay leaves
1	pound green beans, trimmed
6	small carrots, peeled and trimmed
1	Kirby cucumber, peeled and thinly sliced

Stir together vinegar, sugar, salt, coriander, fennel, and
bay leaves in a saucepan over high heat. Bring to a boil,
stirring until sugar has dissolved. Stir in green beans, carrots,
and cucumbers. Remove from heat and let cool completely.
Cover and refrigerate at least overnight or up to 1 week.

German Sausages with Apples, Sauerkraut, and Onion

Half (if not more) of the fun of cooking this main course is seeking out the best of the wursts at your local butcher (or from online purveyors). Use any fully cooked German-style sausage, such as bratwurst, flavored with ginger, nutmeg, and other spices; smoked knockwurst, made with beef or pork; and mild weisswurst with cream, lemon, and cardamom. Store-bought sauerkraut is just fine, but if you are feeling ambitious and want to make your own, visit marthastewart.com for a recipe.

1 to 2 tablespoons safflower or other vegetable oil

12 links assorted fully cooked German sausages, such as bratwurst, knockwurst, and weisswurst

1 large white onion, thinly sliced

2 crisp red apples, such as Gala or Braeburn, cored and cut into 1/2-inch slices

1/4 cup apple cider

1 pound sauerkraut

Assorted mustards, for serving

1. Heat a 12-inch skillet over medium and add 1 tablespoon oil. Halve sausages lengthwise, if desired. Cook until browned and heated through, about 3 to 5 minutes per side. Transfer to a serving platter and cover to keep warm.

2. Add remaining tablespoon oil to skillet if necessary. Add onion and cook until softened, about 3 to 5 minutes. Add apples, stir, and cook until softened, 6 to 7 minutes. Stir in cider and cook for 1 minute. Add sauerkraut and heat until warmed through, about 2 minutes.

3. Transfer sauerkraut mixture to a warm serving platter; serve with sausages and mustards. (Sausages and sauerkraut can be kept warm, covered, in a 250°F oven for up to an hour.)

Warm Potato Salad with Arugula

Tossing a tangy vinaigrette with warm spuds is the formula for a classic German potato salad. But because there's already plenty of meat on this menu, this one features healthy, peppery greens instead of the usual bits of crisp bacon.

3 pounds small red potatoes, scrubbed

3 tablespoons extra-virgin olive oil

Coarse salt and freshly ground pepper

Finely grated zest and 1 tablespoon fresh juice from 1 lemon

1 1/2 teaspoons sherry vinegar

5 ounces spicy greens such as arugula or watercress, washed well and drained, tough stems removed

1. In a large saucepan, bring potatoes to a boil in salted water over high. Reduce to a simmer and cook until tender when pierced with a knife, 15 to 20 minutes. Drain, cool slightly, and halve.

2. Meanwhile, whisk together oil, lemon juice, vinegar, 3/4 teaspoon salt, and 1/4 teaspoon pepper in a bowl.

3. Place warm potato halves in a serving bowl. Add half the vinaigrette and toss to coat. Add greens, lemon zest, and remaining vinaigrette; toss until greens are wilted, and serve immediately.

Pretzel–Crust Ice Cream Pie with Caramel Bourbon Sauce

Instead of setting out a bowl of pretzels before dinner, save the savory snacks for last with this fun twist on dessert. Crush up a bag and use the crumbs to make a press–in crust for ice cream pie. The from–scratch butterscotch sauce picks up the saltiness of the crust and plays off the sweet ice cream filling just beautifully. Chocolate sauce would work well, too.

For crust

6   ounces pretzel twists, crushed (1½ cups), plus more for serving

¼   cup packed light-brown sugar

6   tablespoons unsalted butter, melted

For filling

2   pints vanilla ice cream, well softened

For sauce

1   cup packed light-brown sugar

½   cup (1 stick) unsalted butter

1   vanilla bean, split lengthwise and seeds scraped, or 1 teaspoon pure vanilla extract

⅓   cup heavy cream

1 to 2   tablespoons bourbon, to taste

¼   teaspoon coarse salt

1. Make crust: Preheat oven to 350°F. In a bowl, mix crushed pretzels, sugar, and butter until well combined. Press evenly into bottom and up sides of a 9-inch pie pan. Bake until lightly golden and set, 9 to 12 minutes. Transfer to a wire rack to cool completely.

2. Fill pie: Transfer softened ice cream to cooled crust and spread evenly using an offset spatula. Swoop and swirl as desired. Cover and freeze until set, at least 4 hours and up to overnight.

3. Make sauce: In a saucepan, bring brown sugar, butter, and vanilla bean and seeds to a boil; cook, stirring occasionally, 2 minutes. Remove from heat and add cream, bourbon, and salt. Return to heat, bring to a boil, and cook 30 seconds. Discard the vanilla pod and let cool slightly. (Sauce can be refrigerated up to 1 week; warm over low before serving.) Serve ice cream pie with sauce and additional crushed pretzels.

PREP PLAN

One Week Before

Pickle vegetables

Make sauce for pie

Two Days Before

Prepare pizza dough (if not using store-bought)

One Day Before

Bake pie crust and let cool, then fill and freeze

The Day Of

Scrub potatoes; prep greens for salad

Assemble and bake *flammeküche*

Just Before Guests Arrive

Cook sausages as well as sauerkraut with apples and onion; keep warm in the oven

Boil potatoes

Toss together potato salad; cover to keep warm

Reheat sauce for dessert

TURKEY DAY DINNER

It's likely that sooner or later, the two of you will host Thanksgiving. But honestly, there's no reason to stress over it—or worse, to avoid it. Instead, rise to the delicious occasion. After all, you'll pick up a few new skills, gain kitchen confidence, and put some of your wedding gifts to good use. And ultimately, the whole day can serve as a reminder of your great good fortune in being together. **SERVES 8**

269
GATHER ROUND

The Menu Cognac Sparklers ■ Manhattans ■ Cheese Coins with Pepper Jelly ■ Artichoke and Feta Dip ■ No-Knead Cloverleaf Rolls ■ Herb-Roasted Turkey ■ Stuffing with Mushrooms and Sage ■ Spiced Cranberry Relish ■ Caramelized Chestnuts and Brussels Sprouts ■ Roasted Root Vegetables ■ Duchess Potatoes ■ Maple Nut Tart ■ Indian Pudding ■ Apple-Cranberry Pandowdy

Cognac Sparklers

In this sophisticated cocktail, the apple flavor plays off the strength of the cognac. Hard sparkling cider may be substituted for soft.

1   ounce (2 tablespoons) cognac

1   cup sparkling apple cider, chilled

Bitters

Pour 1 tablespoon cognac into each of 2 champagne flutes. Top each with ½ cup sparkling cider and a few dashes of bitters.

Manhattans

A perfect balance of sweet, bitter, and aromatic, the manhattan is a timeless classic.

2   ounces (¼ cup) rye whiskey or bourbon

1   ounce (2 tablespoons) sweet red vermouth

2   dashes bitters

1   cup ice

Maraschino cherry, for garnish

Combine whiskey, vermouth, and bitters with ice in a cocktail shaker; shake well. Strain into a chilled martini glass. Garnish with a cherry.

Cheese Coins with Pepper Jelly

A staff favorite at Martha Stewart Living, these slice-and-bake crackers make a delicious pre-dinner snack all on their own. Dollop them with hot-pepper jelly, however, and they become instantly ready for any party.

2   cups all-purpose flour, plus more for surface

1   teaspoon salt

1   teaspoon paprika

½   teaspoon cayenne pepper

1   cup (2 sticks) cold unsalted butter, cut into pieces

1   cup grated sharp cheddar cheese (4 ounces)

⅓   cup jalapeño jelly

1. Pulse to blend flour, salt, paprika, and cayenne pepper in a food processor. Add butter; pulse until mixture resembles coarse meal. Add cheese and process until dough just starts to hold together. Turn out dough onto a lightly floured surface. Knead a few times. Divide into 4 equal pieces and roll each into a log about 1 inch in diameter. Wrap in plastic and chill until firm, at least 1 hour and up to 3 days (or freeze for up to 1 month).

2. Preheat oven to 350°F. Line baking sheets with parchment. Slice dough into ⅓-inch-thick rounds and place 2 inches apart on baking sheets. Bake, rotating sheets halfway through, until rounds are lightly browned, about 20 minutes. Let cool on baking sheets 1 minute, then transfer to wire racks. (Coins can be stored up to one week in advance at room temperature.)

3. Heat jelly in a small saucepan over low heat until almost melted, 10 minutes. Spoon jelly onto center of each coin.

Artichoke and Feta Dip

The quickest appetizer on the block: Surround a big piece of feta with artichoke hearts, oregano, and lemon peel. Douse the whole lot in olive oil, heat through, and you're done!

12   ounces sheep's-milk feta

½   cup extra-virgin olive oil

1   can (13.75 ounces) quartered artichoke hearts, drained and cut in half

5   strips lemon zest

1   tablespoon packed fresh oregano leaves

¼   teaspoon red-pepper flakes

     Crackers or crostini, for serving

Preheat oven to 350°F. Place feta in middle of a baking dish. Pour oil over cheese; sprinkle remaining ingredients on and around it. Cover with parchment-lined foil and bake until heated through, about 40 minutes. Let cool slightly before serving with crackers or crostini.

No-Knead Cloverleaf Rolls

Making rolls from scratch may seem like more trouble than it's worth, especially on Thanksgiving. But these rolls are a game changer. True to the name, the dough comes together easily, with no need to knead; you simply form it into balls and bake in muffin tins. And once you start passing a basket of warm-from-the-oven rolls around the table, you're guaranteed to make everyone sitting around it very grateful indeed.

3   tablespoons sugar

1   cup warm water (110°F to 115°F)

1   package (¼ ounce) active dry yeast (2¼ teaspoons)

3   cups all-purpose flour

1½   teaspoons table salt

1   large egg

3   tablespoons unsalted butter, melted and cooled, plus more for brushing

     Vegetable-oil cooking spray

     Coarse salt

1. In a large bowl, combine sugar and water. Sprinkle yeast on top and let sit until foamy, about 5 minutes. Add 1 cup flour and, with an electric mixer, beat on medium until smooth, about 2 minutes. Add table salt, egg, and butter, and beat until combined. Add remaining 2 cups flour and, with a wooden spoon, mix until just combined. Lightly coat a large bowl with cooking spray. Transfer dough to bowl, lightly coat with cooking spray, and loosely cover with plastic wrap. Refrigerate overnight (or up to 2 days). Dough will double in size.

2. Divide dough into 27 equal pieces (1 ounce each). Lightly coat 9 standard muffin cups and your hands with cooking spray. Roll each dough piece into a smooth ball and place 3 balls in each cup. Liberally coat with cooking spray and loosely cover with plastic wrap. Let rise in a warm, draft-free place until doubled, 45 to 90 minutes.

3. Preheat oven to 375°F. Bake rolls until puffed and deep golden, 15 to 20 minutes. Brush with melted butter and sprinkle with coarse salt; serve warm. (To store, let cool, wrap tightly in plastic, and keep at room temperature up to 2 days.)

PREP PLAN

One Week Before

Prepare cranberry relish

Make duchess potatoes and freeze

Two Days Before

Bake cheese coins

Make pie dough for pandowdy and tart

Make roll dough

One Day Before

Chill sparkling cider

Bake rolls

Prepare stuffing and refrigerate in baking dish

Fill and bake maple nut tart

Bake Indian pudding

The Day Of

Roast turkey, then bake stuffing and make gravy

Roast vegetables for side dish

Assemble and bake pandowdy

Just Before Guests Arrive

Whip cream and refrigerate

Bake feta dip

Cook chestnut and brussels sprouts side dish

Bake duchess potatoes

During Dinner

Reheat Indian pudding

Herb-Roasted Turkey

Over the years, we've cooked many hundreds of turkeys at Martha Stewart Living, testing and trying out every technique you can think of. This foolproof recipe is among the easiest and tastiest. It's also perfect for anyone who has never cooked a Thanksgiving meal before. What intimidates most cooks is how to roast the whole bird without drying out the meat, especially the breast. Here the liquid in the bottom of the roasting pan keeps the meat moist as it cooks. Apple cider adds a little sweetness, too. If you prefer, you can substitute water for the cider.

1	turkey (about 12 pounds), thawed if frozen, rinsed and patted dry
½	cup chopped fresh flat-leaf parsley
1	tablespoon chopped fresh rosemary, plus 3 sprigs
1	tablespoon chopped fresh sage leaves
1½	teaspoons chopped fresh thyme leaves
8	garlic cloves, finely chopped (3 tablespoons)
5	tablespoons olive oil
	Coarse salt and freshly ground pepper
2	lemons, poked all over with a fork
1	quart apple cider

1. Preheat oven to 350°F with rack in lowest position. Remove giblets and neck from turkey cavity. Discard liver. Rinse giblets and neck; refrigerate until ready to make broth for gravy.

2. Turn turkey on its back and bend wing tips forward and underneath neck cavity of bird so they stay in place (you may have to break the bones).

3. In a small bowl, combine parsley, chopped rosemary, sage, thyme, garlic, 4 tablespoons oil, 1 teaspoon salt, and ½ teaspoon pepper. Gently slip your fingers between skin and meat of breast and around thighs. Evenly spread herb mixture under skin of both, starting with thigh area and working toward neck.

4. Season cavity with salt and pepper, and loosely fill with lemons and rosemary sprigs. Using cotton kitchen twine, tie legs together so bird retains its shape during cooking.

5. Pour cider in bottom of pan. Set roasting rack on top. Lift turkey onto rack, breast side up; rub with remaining tablespoon oil; season generously with salt and pepper. Tent turkey loosely with foil. Roast 1 hour. Uncover and continue to roast, basting frequently with pan juices, until an instant-read thermometer inserted into thickest part of thigh (avoiding bone) registers 170°F, 2½ to 3 hours more. (Temperature will rise about 10 degrees as turkey rests.) Tent with foil if browning too quickly; add water if pan becomes dry. Cover loosely with foil and let stand 30 minutes before carving.

WHITE-WINE GRAVY

	14 cups cold water
	Neck and giblets from turkey (see recipe above)
1	carrot, cut into 2 or 3 pieces
1	onion, cut into 2 or 3 pieces
1	stalk celery, cut into 2 or 3 pieces
	Small handful of flat-leaf parsley sprigs and stems
1	bay leaf
5	whole black peppercorns
	Roasting pan with turkey drippings (see recipe above)
1	cup dry white wine
½	cup all-purpose flour
	Coarse salt and freshly ground pepper

1. While the turkey roasts, combine 10 cups water with neck, giblets, carrot, onion, celery, parsley, bay leaf, and peppercorns in a large stockpot and bring to a boil. Reduce heat and simmer, skimming froth off top occasionally, until reduced by half, about 1 hour. Pour through a fine-mesh sieve into a bowl; discard solids. (You should have about 5 cups stock.)

2. While the turkey rests, pour juices from roasting pan into a fat separator, reserving pan. (You can also use a large liquid-measuring cup. Let stand 10 minutes; skim off fat.) Place the roasting pan on the stove across two burners. Heat drippings over medium-high, scraping up browned bits, until thickened, about 10 minutes.

3. Add wine; cook, stirring constantly, until syrupy, 5 to 6 minutes. Gradually whisk in flour, and cook, whisking constantly, until incorporated, about 1 minute. Gradually add 1 cup stock; cook, whisking, until flour is a deep caramel color, 2 to 3 minutes.

4. Gradually stir in 3 more cups stock and remaining 4 cups water. Bring to a simmer; cook, stirring occasionally, until gravy reaches desired thickness, 10 to 15 minutes. Strain gravy through a fine-mesh sieve; discard solids. Season generously with salt and pepper, and serve.

Stuffing with Mushrooms and Sage

The great thing about stuffing is that it's almost impossible to mess up: A little more of this or less of that won't affect the results too much. The key is having just the right amount of liquid to keep the stuffing moist but not soggy. And as for whether to stuff or not to stuff the bird? That's a matter of preference, but if it's your first time hosting the meal, keep things simple by cooking the stuffing outside of the turkey. You can also do a few things ahead of time to shorten your task list on game day, like drying out the bread cubes and cooking the vegetables up through step 3.

- 2 loaves Italian bread (about 10 ounces each), torn into bite-size pieces
- 4 tablespoons butter, room temperature, plus more for baking dish and foil
- 4 celery stalks, thinly sliced
- 4 shallots, minced
- 2 garlic cloves, minced
  Coarse salt and freshly ground pepper
- 1 pound chopped mixed mushrooms
- ¼ teaspoon dried rubbed sage
- ½ cup dry white wine
- ½ cup fresh flat-leaf parsley leaves, chopped
- 3 large eggs, lightly beaten
- 2 cans (14.5 ounces each) low-sodium chicken broth

1. Preheat oven to 400°F. Arrange bread in a single layer on 2 rimmed baking sheets. Bake, rotating sheets halfway through, until crisp but not browned, about 10 minutes.

2. In a large saucepan, melt butter over medium heat. Add celery, shallots, and garlic; season with salt and pepper. Cook, stirring occasionally, until vegetables are softened, 5 to 7 minutes.

Stir in mushrooms and sage. Cook until liquid released from mushrooms has evaporated, 5 to 7 minutes. Add wine and cook until evaporated, 3 to 5 minutes. Transfer to a large bowl.

3. Add bread, parsley, and eggs to a bowl. Season with 1½ teaspoons salt and ¼ teaspoon pepper; stir to combine. Mix in half of broth. Continue to add in more broth until stuffing is just moistened but not wet (there should not be any liquid in the bottom of the bowl). Spoon stuffing into a buttered baking dish. Cover with buttered aluminum foil and refrigerate.

4. When turkey is removed from oven to rest, place covered pan in oven and bake until cooked through, 25 to 30 minutes. Uncover and bake until golden, about 15 minutes more.

Spiced Cranberry Relish

The spices in this tangy sauce go well with turkey. It's easy to double a batch, and it also keeps well so you can make it up to a week ahead of Thanksgiving. Cranberries contain lots of pectin, which is released in cooking; when sugar is added, the tart juices thicken and give the sauce body.

- 1 bag (12 ounces) fresh or frozen cranberries
- ½ cup packed dark-brown sugar
- 1 cup water
- 1 tablespoon finely grated peeled fresh ginger
- ⅛ teaspoon ground cloves

In a saucepan, bring cranberries, sugar, water, ginger, and cloves to a boil over high. Reduce heat and simmer, stirring occasionally, until cranberries have burst and sauce is slightly thickened, about 10 minutes. Remove from heat and let cool to room temperature. (Refrigerate in an airtight container up to 1 week. Bring to room temperature before serving.)

ROASTED VEGETABLES 101

Nothing quite makes the case for simple cooking like roasted vegetables. With just salt, pepper, a bit of oil, and a hot oven, nearly every vegetable becomes something sublime. Their flavors are intensified and concentrated, with a sweetness that only roasting can impart. Once you learn the basic technique, don't be timid about experimenting with seasonal combinations.

■ Use shallow pans (rimmed baking sheets are perfect) and don't overcrowd vegetables. Roast them in a single layer. This allows them to brown and caramelize evenly rather than steam.

■ Toss vegetables during roasting; they'll stay coated with oil and won't dry out. And rotate the pan halfway through.

■ Roasting times will depend on the vegetables; if using both slow- and quick-roasting vegetables together, cut the slow-roasting ones in smaller pieces than the quick-roasting ones so they'll all be done at the same time.

277

Caramelized Chestnuts and Brussels Sprouts

In this easy preparation, luxurious roasted chestnuts are paired with brussels sprouts that have been sautéed in butter until tender and golden. Cider vinegar is reduced to a glaze that gives the whole dish unbeatable flavor and tang.

2	tablespoons unsalted butter
1	tablespoon olive oil
2	pounds brussels sprouts, trimmed and cut in half
	Coarse salt and freshly ground pepper
2	cups vacuum-packed whole cooked chestnuts
1/2	cup cider vinegar
1/4	cup sugar
1/4	cup low-sodium chicken broth or turkey stock

1. Melt butter and oil in a large sauté pan set over medium-high heat. Add brussels sprouts, and season with salt and pepper. Cook, stirring occasionally, until golden, 16 to 18 minutes.

2. Add chestnuts; cook, gently stirring occasionally, until sprouts are tender and spotted deep brown, 20 to 25 minutes. Add vinegar, sugar, and broth. Cook, stirring occasionally, until liquid has reduced to a syrup, 4 to 5 minutes. Transfer to a serving dish.

Roasted Root Vegetables

2	pounds acorn squash, sliced into wedges
2	pounds rutabaga, peeled and cut into wedges
1	pound parsnip, peeled and cut into half-moons
1	pound celery root, peeled and coarsely chopped
1	pound red onion, sliced
1/4	cup olive oil
	Coarse salt and freshly ground pepper
6	thyme sprigs

1. Preheat oven to 450°F. Divide vegetables between 2 rimmed baking sheets. Dividing evenly, toss with oil, 2 teaspoons coarse salt, 1/4 teaspoon pepper, and thyme sprigs.

2. Roast, tossing them and rotating sheets from top to bottom halfway through, until vegetables are tender and beginning to brown, about 50 minutes. Serve hot or at room temperature.

Duchess Potatoes

The name of these soft, buttery spuds with crisp, golden crusts sounds regal, but they're not much more complicated to make than everyday mashed potatoes (like the ones on page 122, which you can substitute here if you wish). Duchess potatoes are often piped into mounds, but we've simplified things by shaping them with a spoon. The indented centers are made to hold pools of gravy or butter (yes, please!). And the beauty of this recipe is that you can make the single servings in advance, transfer to a resealable bag, and freeze them, freeing you up on Thanksgiving morning.

2½	pounds Yukon Gold potatoes (about 10 medium), peeled and cut into 1-inch pieces
	Coarse salt and freshly ground pepper
3	tablespoons cold unsalted butter, plus more for parchment
3	large egg yolks
1/4	cup plus 2 teaspoons heavy cream
	Pinch of freshly grated nutmeg
	Thyme sprigs, for garnish

1. In a large pot, cover potatoes with cold salted water by 2 inches. Bring to a boil; reduce to a rapid simmer and cook until tender, about 15 minutes. Drain in a colander; let sit 5 minutes, then return to pot. Add butter and, with a potato masher, mash until smooth. Season with salt and pepper. Add 2 egg yolks, 1/4 cup cream, and nutmeg; stir until combined.

2. Preheat oven to 450°F. Line a rimmed baking sheet with parchment and lightly butter paper. Dollop mixture into 8 equal portions on sheet, 2 inches apart. Using the back of a spoon, create a small well in the center of each. Freeze until firm, about 15 minutes. Whisk together remaining egg yolk and 2 teaspoons cream. Brush egg wash on potatoes and bake until golden, about 15 minutes. Before serving, garnish with thyme.

Maple Nut Tart

This spin on pecan pie adds walnuts to the mix and features maple syrup instead of corn syrup, lending deeper, richer flavor to an of-the-season treat.

	All-purpose flour, for surface
½	recipe Pie Dough (page 283)
2	large eggs
¼	cup packed light-brown sugar
¼	teaspoon salt
1	cup pure maple syrup
1½	cups coarsely chopped pecans
1½	cups coarsely chopped walnuts
	Lightly sweetened softly whipped cream (recipe follows) or vanilla ice cream, for serving

1. Preheat oven to 350°F. Line a rimmed baking sheet with parchment. On a lightly floured surface, roll out dough to an 11-inch round. Fit into bottom and up sides of a 9-inch tart pan with a removable bottom. Trim excess dough flush with rim.

2. In a bowl, whisk together eggs, sugar, and salt; whisk in maple syrup. Add nuts and mix to combine thoroughly. Place tart pan on prepared sheet and pour in filling. Bake until filling is set and crust is lightly golden, 55 to 60 minutes. Transfer to a wire rack and let cool completely in pan before unmolding. Serve with whipped cream or ice cream.

LIGHTLY SWEETENED WHIPPED CREAM

2	cups heavy cream, chilled
2	tablespoons confectioners' sugar

With an electric mixer on medium-high speed (or by hand), whisk cream in a well-chilled bowl until soft peaks form. Add sugar, and whisk just until medium-stiff peaks form (do not overmix). Whipped cream can be refrigerated in an airtight container for up to 2 hours.

Indian Pudding

It's time for this Colonial era dessert to make a comeback. The classic New England corn-and-molasses spoonbread is definitely not as widely known today as it should be. It's scrumptious and comforting, and is very easy to make with just a handful of pantry ingredients. (And it's gluten-free!) If you ever tried it as a kid, one bite should help the memories come flooding back; if not, prepare for a new favorite. The sweet, cold richness of whipped cream or vanilla ice cream perfectly balances the deep dark, nearly burnt flavor of the pudding.

4	cups half-and-half
¾	cup unsulfured molasses
4	tablespoons unsalted butter, plus more for dish
1	teaspoon ground ginger
1	teaspoon ground cinnamon
1	teaspoon salt
½	cup yellow cornmeal
	Lightly sweetened softly whipped cream or vanilla ice cream, for serving

1. Preheat oven to 275°F. In a saucepan, combine half-and-half, molasses, butter, ginger, cinnamon, and salt. Bring to a boil, stirring to combine. Remove from heat and whisk in cornmeal until batter is smooth.

2. Transfer mixture to a buttered 8-inch square baking dish and bake until pudding is firm but still jiggles slightly in the center when gently shaken, 2 to 2½ hours. Let cool 30 minutes. Serve warm or at room temperature, topped with whipped cream or ice cream.

Apple-Cranberry Pandowdy

Here's another old-fashioned dessert that deserves a prominent place on the modern table. Pandowdy is way more forgiving than a double-crust pie—in fact, a big part of its charm lies in its rustic imprecision. You can cut the dough that covers the top into a bunch of squares (or other shapes), as we've done here, or you can simply drape it over the top and slash a few vents in it (this allows steam to escape and keeps the crust from getting soggy). It's worth seeking out two varieties of apples if you can: Firm but tender Rome holds its shape, while creamy McIntosh cooks down into a sauce.

For pie dough

2½ cups all-purpose flour

1 teaspoon salt

1 teaspoon sugar

1 cup (2 sticks) unsalted butter, cold and cut into small pieces

¼ to ½ cup ice water

For filling

3 Rome apples (1½ pounds), peeled, cored, and cut into ½-inch slices

4 McIntosh apples (1½ pounds), peeled, cored, and cut into ½-inch slices

1 cup cranberries (thawed if frozen)

⅓ cup packed light-brown sugar

1 tablespoon fresh lemon juice

3 tablespoons all-purpose flour

½ teaspoon salt

2 tablespoons unsalted butter, cut into pieces

1 tablespoon heavy cream

2 teaspoons sanding sugar

Lightly sweetened whipped cream or vanilla ice cream, for serving

1. Make the pie dough: In the bowl of a food processor, combine flour, salt, and sugar (or whisk together by hand in a bowl). Add butter, and process until the mixture resembles coarse meal, 8 to 10 seconds (or quickly cut in with a pastry blender or your fingertips). On a floured piece of parchment, roll out dough to ⅛-inch thickness. Refrigerate until firm, about 20 minutes.

2. Drizzle ¼ cup water over mixture. Pulse (or mix with a fork) until dough just begins to hold together. To test, squeeze a small amount: If it is crumbly, add up to ¼ cup more ice water, 1 tablespoon at a time.

3. Divide dough in half onto two pieces of plastic wrap. Gather into two balls, wrap loosely in plastic, and press each into a disk. Refrigerate until firm, well wrapped in plastic, 1 hour or up to overnight. (Dough may be frozen, for up to 1 month; thaw in refrigerator before using.)

4. Make the filling: Preheat oven to 375°F. In a large bowl, toss together apples, cranberries, brown sugar, lemon juice, flour, and salt. Transfer to a 2-quart baking pan and dot with butter. With a pastry whee or sharp knife, cut dough into pieces about 3 inches square. Lay dough pieces, overlapping slightly, on top of apple mixture. Brush dough with cream and sprinkle with sanding sugar. Bake until crust is browned and juices are bubbling, about 1 hour. Let cool at least 15 minutes. Serve warm or at room temperature with whipped cream or ice cream.

HOLIDAY COCKTAILS

Inspired by spy movies and Cold War thrillers, we've devised a spread of seriously sophisticated snacks and cocktails: smoked fishes on black bread, buckwheat blini with caviar and crème fraîche, and a little   make that lots of—vodka and champagne. Bite-size desserts (chocolate truffles, mini cheesecakes, and more) ensure a sweet late-night send-off. **SERVES 10**

The Menu Juniper Champagne Sparklers ▪ Dill-Vodka Martinis ▪ Beet-and-Lemon Shrub Cocktails ▪ Potato and Beet Latkes ▪ Brown Butter-Herbed Cashews ▪ Parsnip Chips with Roast Beef and Horseradish Cream ▪ Buttered Rye with Gravlax and Slaw ▪ Buckwheat Blini with Caviar and Crème Fraîche ▪ Chocolate Truffles ▪ Pinched Orange Macaroons ▪ Mini Cheesecakes

Juniper Champagne Sparklers

A simple syrup infused with juniper berries adds citrusy-green notes to glasses of bubbly, while a fragrant swizzle of pine plays right along.

½	cup sugar
1½	cups water
¼	cup juniper berries, crushed
1	bottle (750 ml) champagne or prosecco
	Unsprayed pine sprigs, for serving (optional)

1. Bring sugar, water, and juniper berries to a simmer in a saucepan over medium heat, stirring until sugar is dissolved. Remove from heat; let cool completely. Strain through a fine-mesh sieve; discard solids. Refrigerate at least 1 hour (or up to 1 week).

2. For each cocktail, combine 3 tablespoons juniper syrup with ½ cup sparkling wine in a glass. Garnish with a pine sprig, if desired; serve immediately.

Dill-Vodka Martinis

Look for dill vodka at your local liquor store, or consider making your own flavored vodkas (see page 288); garnish accordingly.

3	cups dill-infused vodka
⅓	cup dry vermouth
1	Kirby cucumber, sliced, for serving
	Capers, for serving
	Dill sprigs, for serving

To make a pitcher, mix vodka with vermouth. Add ice and stir. Strain into chilled martini glasses and serve with sliced cucumbers, capers, and dill.

Beet-and-Lemon Shrub Cocktails

This drink comes from Russ & Daughters Café, on Manhattan's Lower East Side, famous for its delectable smoked fish and caviar platters. For the beet juice, you will need a juicer—or to visit a juice bar. To make mocktails, simply leave out the vodka and top with seltzer.

For shrub

5	cups water
2	tablespoons distilled white vinegar
½	cup sugar
1	cup fresh beet juice
1	cup fresh lemon juice

For cocktails

12	ounces vodka
24	ounces seltzer
	Pickled green tomatoes or other vegetables, for garnish (optional)

1. Make shrub: Whisk together ¾ cup water, the vinegar, and sugar until sugar is dissolved. Combine remaining water, the beet juice, and lemon juice, and mix well. Stir in vinegar mixture. Refrigerate 48 hours before using.

2. Make cocktails: Mix together shrub and vodka. Fill glasses with ice. Top off with seltzer and garnish with pickled vegetables. Serve immediately.

INFUSED VODKAS

Making your own flavored vodkas can be a whole lot tastier—and more fun—than picking up a bottle at the liquor store. Try any combination of ingredients below with 1½ cups vodka, or experiment with custom blends. Combine ingredients in an airtight jar, and store in a cool, dark place for a few days, shaking occasionally—then strain and start sipping. Vodkas keep at room temperature for up to 1 month or frozen up to 2 months, unless otherwise indicated.

Beet + Horseradish
Infuse vodka with ½ sliced small beet and 3 thin slices peeled fresh horseradish for 2 days. (Store for up to 2 weeks or freeze for up to 1 month.) Serve a shot of these classic Russian flavors with simple syrup and a splash of seltzer.

Fennel + Lemon
Infuse vodka with 2 sprigs fennel fronds and 2 thin lemon slices for 2 days. Serve on the rocks, or mix with tonic and a squeeze of lemon.

Celery + Bay Leaf
Infuse vodka with ½ celery stalk, 2 celery leaves, and 1 dried bay leaf for 2 days. Use in a Bloody Mary, or mix with dry sherry and seltzer for a savory-sweet fizz.

Grapefruit Zest + Coriander
Infuse vodka with 2 strips grapefruit zest and 1 tablespoon toasted coarsely ground coriander seeds for 3 days. Serve as an extra zip of spiced citrus in a Salty Dog, or mix with sparkling lemonade.

Potato and Beet Latkes

Put a little swirl in your latkes by slicing the vegetables (here potato and beet) into strips with a spiralizer. You can also grate them the old-fashioned way on the large holes of a box grater, or with the grating disk of a food processor.

- 2 medium potatoes, peeled, halved, and sliced on a turning slicer, or coarsely grated
- 2 medium beets, peeled and sliced on a turning slicer, or coarsely grated
- 2 teaspoons coarse salt
- 1 large egg, lightly beaten

  Safflower or other vegetable oil, for frying
- 4 ounces fresh goat cheese, for serving
- ½ cup black olives, pitted and cut into slivers, for serving

  Fresh thyme leaves, for garnish

1. In a large bowl, toss vegetables with 1½ teaspoons salt. Divide potato-beet mixture into 2 batches on clean kitchen towels and squeeze out excess liquid. Transfer all vegetables to a bowl and mix to combine with egg and remaining ½ teaspoon salt.

2. Fill a large nonstick skillet with about ½ inch oil and heat over medium; it's ready when a bit of potato-beet mixture sizzles when added. Working in batches, carefully drop 2 tablespoons potato-beet mixture into oil for each latke, pressing to flatten. Cook until crisp and golden, about 4 minutes per side, adjusting heat as needed. Drain on paper towels and serve warm, each topped with a dollop of goat cheese and a few black olive slivers. (Latkes can be kept warm in a 250°F oven until ready to top and serve.)

Brown Butter—Herbed Cashews

Try any combination of nuts in this recipe—almonds, walnuts, pecans, and such. A big bowl filled with seasoned cashews feels especially luxurious.

- 10 cups unsalted raw cashews
- 4 tablespoons unsalted butter
- 3 tablespoons light-brown sugar
- 2½ teaspoons coarse salt
- 1 teaspoon freshly ground black pepper
- ½ teaspoon cayenne pepper
- 5 sprigs thyme
- 2 sprigs rosemary

1. Preheat oven to 350°F. Place cashews in a single layer on a rimmed baking sheet and toast until brown and fragrant, 10 to 15 minutes.

2. Meanwhile, melt butter in a small saucepan over medium-high heat. Continue cooking until butter becomes fragrant and golden brown, 8 to 10 minutes, taking care not to burn. Remove from heat.

3. In a large bowl, mix together brown sugar, salt, black pepper, cayenne pepper, thyme, and rosemary; mix in brown butter. Add nuts and toss to combine. Return nuts to sheet and transfer to oven. Bake until nuts are semidry, about 10 minutes. Remove from oven and let cool completely before serving.

Parsnip Chips with Roast Beef and Horseradish Cream

Feel free to substitute store-bought root chips in place of the parsnip ones, or even your favorite thick-cut potato chips.

6 large parsnips, peeled and sliced into 1/8-inch-thick rounds

1 tablespoon olive oil

Coarse salt and freshly ground pepper

1/2 cup sour cream

3 tablespoons grated peeled fresh horseradish

1 tablespoon distilled white vinegar

1/4 pound sliced roast beef, cut into bite-size pieces

1. Preheat oven to 425°F. In a bowl, toss parsnips with oil, then arrange in a single layer on 2 large rimmed baking sheets. Season well with salt and pepper. Roast until soft and golden, about 20 minutes. Turn off oven and leave parsnips to crisp, 5 to 7 minutes.

2. Whisk together sour cream, horseradish, vinegar, and 1/2 teaspoon salt in a bowl. Cover and refrigerate up to 1 day. Stir before serving.

3. Top each chip with a dollop of horseradish cream and a piece of roast beef. Or set out bowls of all three and let guests build their own.

Buttered Rye with Gravlax and Slaw

A perfect balance of salt, salmon, and spice makes Scandinavian gravlax delicious at any time of year, but its flavors are particularly well-suited to the winter holidays. Here we've topped slices of dark rye with a thick schmear of butter, followed by thin slices of the cured fish and some cool, crunchy slaw. You can find gravlax at specialty-food stores, or substitute smoked salmon. If you feel like making your own (waiting for it to cure for three days is really the only difficult step), you can find Martha's foolproof recipe at marthastewart.com.

For slaw

1/2 cup plain yogurt

1 seeded and finely chopped fresh red chile

1 tablespoon cider vinegar

1 tablespoon minced peeled fresh ginger

1 teaspoon black mustard seeds, toasted

1 teaspoon coarse salt

1/4 teaspoon cumin seeds, toasted

3 cups shredded cabbage

1 Granny Smith apple, cut into matchsticks

For canapés

1/2 cup (1 stick) unsalted butter, room temperature

6 slices dark rye bread, cut into thirds

6 ounces thinly sliced gravlax

1. Make slaw: In a bowl, whisk together yogurt, chile, vinegar, ginger, mustard seeds, salt, and cumin seeds. Stir in cabbage and apples. Refrigerate for 30 minutes and up to 8 hours before serving.

2. Make canapés: Spread a layer of butter on each bread piece, then top with sliced gravlax and slaw.

NOSH 101

For a party like this, we recommend offering a selection of breads (such as rye and pumpernickel, crispbreads, and bagel chips), spreads (plain and scallion cream cheeses and fish salads), smoked fish, and garnishes (capers, minced chives, sliced tomatoes, and diced red onion or scallions). Find a good delicatessen or other specialty shop, nearby or online: Russ & Daughters (russanddaughters .com) has an excellent selection of caviar and smoked fish. Cut breads into small squares, rounds, or triangles. Here are a few favorite combinations:

■ Dark rye with sieved (mimosa) hard-cooked egg and chopped cornichons

■ Pumpernickel with butter and pickled vegetables (thinly sliced dilly beans or green tomatoes, or finely chopped cauliflower)

■ Swedish crispbread with pickled herring and slivered onion

■ Wheat crackers with whitefish salad, diced red onion, and capers

■ Bagel chips with scallion cream cheese, sliced Nova lox, and trout roe

■ Rye with cream cheese, flaked kippered salmon, sliced tomato, and capers

Buckwheat Blini with Caviar and Crème Fraîche

The Russian buckwheat pancakes known as blini are a world apart from American flapjacks. Served with spoonfuls of crème fraîche and caviar (or sliced smoked fish), they make wonderful hors d'oeuvres alongside glasses of chilled vodka and champagne.

1	package (¼ ounce) active dry yeast (2¼ teaspoons)
½	cup warm water (110°F)
½	cup buckwheat flour
½	cup all-purpose flour
½	teaspoon coarse salt
¾	cup plain yogurt

1	tablespoon unsalted butter, melted
½	teaspoon sugar
2	large eggs, separated
1 to 3	ounces caviar, for serving
	Crème fraîche, for serving
	Fresh dill, for serving

1. Sprinkle yeast over warm water in a small bowl; let stand until foamy, about 7 minutes. Sift flours and salt together into a bowl. Stir together yogurt, butter, sugar, and yolks in a large bowl; whisk in yeast mixture and flour mixture. Let batter stand, covered, in a warm place for 30 minutes.

2. Beat whites until stiff peaks form; fold whites into batter. Let stand 10 minutes.

3. Heat a 12-inch nonstick skillet or crepe pan over medium. Add 1 tablespoon batter; cook blini, 3 or 4 at a time, flipping once, until golden, about 2 minutes per side. Serve with caviar, crème fraîche, and dill.

CAVIAR 101

Not all caviar is created equal. If you dismiss caviar as gritty or too salty, it's possible that the type you tried wasn't the highest quality, because a good caviar—fresh, carefully stored, and served just right—should be a revelation. Traditionally, caviar is derived from three types of sturgeon: beluga, osetra, and sevruga. Because overfishing is threatening the sturgeon population in most of the world, the most responsible choice is American-farmed caviar.

Caviar is extremely perishable and must be refrigerated from the moment it's taken from the fish until it's eaten. Pasteurized caviar is roe that has been partially cooked, thereby giving the eggs a slightly different texture and a longer shelf life. Pressed caviar is composed of damaged eggs and a combination of several different roes.

Store caviar in the coldest part of the refrigerator at 26°F to 36°F. Once opened, it should be consumed within a week. You can store an unopened tin of fresh caviar for two to three weeks, while pasteurized caviar can last for three to four months before opening. When serving, choose bowls and utensils made of nonreactive materials such as glass, plastic, or wood. Traditionally, caviar is served with tiny gold or mother-of-pearl spoons. Always avoid using easily oxidized metals, such as silver or inexpensive stainless steel, which will react with the caviar, giving it a metallic taste.

Chocolate Truffles

Undeniably elegant but simple to create, truffles can be rolled in any number of finishes. Unsweetened cocoa powder is classic, but for variety, roll some in confectioners' sugar, chopped nuts, cocoa nibs, crushed peppermints, or toasted coconut flakes. Similarly, try flavoring the ganache base with spirits, like brandy, whiskey, or rum (6 tablespoons liquor per cup of cream).

8   ounces dark chocolate, finely chopped

     Coarse salt

1   cup heavy cream

     Unsweetened Dutch-process cocoa powder

1. Place chocolate and a pinch of salt in a heatproof bowl. Bring cream just to a boil and pour over chocolate. Let stand, without stirring, 10 minutes. Then stir, scraping sides and bottom of bowl with a flexible spatula, until smooth and shiny.

2. Refrigerate mixture, covered, until firm, at least 4 hours. Use a small ice cream scoop or tablespoon to scoop mixture, and roll into balls. Roll each ball in cocoa. Refrigerate at least 30 minutes or up to 4 days.

Pinched Orange Macaroons

This recipe, one of Martha's favorites, was originally developed by pastry chef Patrick Lemble. The cookies are gluten-free, and they keep well, so they're a great bake-ahead dessert option for entertaining.

2   large egg whites

1   pound almond paste

1/2   cup confectioners' sugar, plus more for rolling

1/8   teaspoon pure almond extract

1   tablespoon Grand Marnier or other orange liqueur

1 1/2 teaspoons finely grated orange zest

1. With an electric mixer, beat 1 egg white, the almond paste, confectioners' sugar, and almond extract on medium until creamy, 2 minutes. Add liqueur and zest, and beat until combined, 1 minute.

2. Turn out dough onto a surface lightly dusted with confectioners' sugar and roll into two 18-inch logs. Slice each log crosswise into 1/2-inch pieces. Roll each piece into a ball. Lightly beat remaining egg white. Brush onto each ball and roll in confectioners' sugar, tapping to remove excess. Transfer to parchment-lined baking sheets. Let stand 30 minutes.

3. Preheat oven to 350°F. Gently pinch each piece of dough to form an irregular pyramid shape. Bake until pale golden, about 15 minutes. Transfer baking sheets to wire racks and let cool completely. (Macaroons can be stored at room temperature for up to 1 week.)

Mini Cheesecakes

1   cup crumbled chocolate-wafer cookies (18 cookies)

1/2   cup plus 1 1/2 tablespoons sugar

3   tablespoons unsalted butter, melted

1   pound cream cheese, room temperature

1/2   teaspoon pure vanilla extract

2   large eggs, lightly beaten

1/2   cup sour cream

       Pinch of salt

1   cup apricot jam

1. Preheat oven to 350°F. Line 2 24-cup miniature muffin tins with paper liners. Mix cookies and 1 tablespoon plus 1 teaspoon sugar in a bowl. Stir in butter. Press 3/4 teaspoon mixture in bottom of each liner. Bake until set, about 7 minutes. Let cool in tins on wire racks.

2. Reduce oven to 275°F. Beat cream cheese with a mixer on medium until smooth. Add remaining 1/2 cup sugar, then vanilla. With mixer running, add eggs slowly, scraping down side of bowl. Add sour cream and salt. Pour 1 tablespoon batter into muffin cups, filling almost to the tops. Bake until sides are set but centers are wobbly, 12 to 15 minutes. Let cool in tins on wire racks. Then wrap tins tightly with plastic and refrigerate 4 hours or overnight. (Cheesecakes will keep, refrigerated, up to 3 days.)

3. Melt jam in a saucepan; strain through a sieve. Spoon 1/2 teaspoon jam on top of each cake.

THANKS.

A book such as this requires a strong commitment on the part of everyone involved, and the team who put it together was committed every step of the way, from the earliest planning stages all the way through to publication. Led by our longtime editorial director of books, Ellen Morrissey, and managing editor, Susanne Ruppert, they worked tirelessly to produce a practical guide to a subject we've never covered before (and with nearly one hundred books published, that's no small feat). Together the team and I set out to demystify the process of cooking together as a couple, and learning to have fun as you do so. Michael McCormick, design director of *Martha Stewart Weddings*, worked diligently and cheerfully to create the beautiful design, including the vibrant layouts with all-new photography. We were delighted that our very talented friend Stephen Kent Johnson agreed to shoot every gorgeous image and that the always inspired and inspiring food stylist Frances Boswell contributed her considerable talents as well. Stylist Megan Hedgpeth selected just the right prop for every photograph and was instrumental in setting the visual tone of the book and the recipes within it—from everyday meals for two to those special days and nights when the table is surrounded by an untold number of family and friends.

Several excellent writers and editors, including Salma Abdelnour, Evelyn Battaglia, Bridget Fitzgerald, Jane Lear, Nanette Maxim, and Fan Winston, contributed to the voluminous text. Ava Pollack and Christopher Rudolph assisted the editorial team at various stages. John Myers, Mike Varrassi, Stacey Tyrell, and Jeanine Robinson each helped make the book and its photographs look as good as they do. Denise Ginley assisted with the food on all the photo shoots, and Anne Eastman lent her artful eye to the prop styling. Caitlin Brown and Kavita Thirupuvanam tested recipes for us, and Gertrude Porter, Josefa Palacios, and Aida Ibarra kept the kitchens running smoothly and efficiently. We thank those in Martha Stewart Living's food department, led by Sarah Carey, who offered invaluable guidance and expertise.

Of our nearly one hundred books, all but one has been published by Clarkson/Potter, an imprint of the Crown Publishing Group, a division of Penguin Random House, a subsidiary of Bertelsmann. This represents a thirty-five-year partnership with our publisher, and we are especially proud of that longstanding relationship and the commitment it represents. We are grateful to all the members of the Clarkson/Potter team at Crown who continue to collaborate with us in our book publishing efforts, including (but surely not limited to) Rica Allannic, Jana Branson, Doris Cooper, Terry Deal, Debbie Glasserman, Linnea Knollmueller, Maya Mavjee, Mark McCauslin, Ashley Phillips Meyer, Marysarah Quinn, Kate Tyler, Stephanie Davis, and Aaron Wehner.

INDEX

D

Index

Index

PAELLA PARTY

Paella is one of the great one-pot wonders of the world. After all, what could be better for a fun dinner party than one big pan in the center of the table, filled with golden rice and beautifully briny, salty-sweet shellfish? Maybe a pitcher or two of sangria, a few tapas, and a few more friends. **SERVES 8**